PROJECT REWIRE

new media from the inside out

SELECTED AND
INTRODUCED BY

Judy Daubenmier

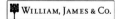
WILLIAM, JAMES & CO.

Wilsonville, Oregon
www.wmjasco.com

> *To the News Hounds*
> —J.D.

Publisher   Jim Leisy (james_leisy@wmjasco.com)

Series Editor   Tom Sumner

Printed in the U.S.A.

William, James & Co. is an imprint of Franklin, Beedle & Associates, Inc.
pp. 54–60:

Library of Congress Cataloging in Publication data

Project rewire : new media from the inside out / selected and introduced by Judy Daubenmier.
      p. cm.
      ISBN 1-59028-051-2
   1. Television broadcasting of news—United States. 2. Online journalism—United States. I. Daubenmier, Judy.
PN4888.T4P7 2006
070.4'30973—dc22

                                                          2006020140

CONTENTS

CHAPTER ONE

Unwired:
how the media got disconnected
by Judy Daubenmier

page 1

CHAPTER TWO

The great rewiring:
internet media covers the media

page 45

CONTENTS

CONTENTS

FOREWORD

TV CONSULTANTS telling anchors that the most important part of covering a tragedy is what to wear on set. Conservative critics who cow journalists into "proving" they're not really liberal. Local stories of disappearing white women on the national news. Greedy executives demanding outrageous profit margins and cutting newsrooms when papers don't produce. Such is the picture painted in this book by Judy Daubenmier, a journalist and researcher on *Outfoxed: Rupert Murdoch's War on Journalism*.

Daubenmier collects the work of some of the most important press critics working today. Bloggers and journalists, they take us through the most important blunders of the mass media, from the 2000 election to the war in Iraq. It's a litany of missteps, fraught with instances of laziness, lies and manipulation, that leaves the reader with an overwhelming picture of a Fourth Estate for sale.

Surprisingly, this isn't a hopeless situation, nor are its chroniclers cynical. Daubenmier and the critics she gathers in this volume point out media mistakes not out of a desire to point and laugh, but out of a hunger for a return to the role the press once provided: watchdogs of government and representatives of the people.

They criticize because they believe very deeply in the value of good reporting and good reporters, and that belief shines through every piece in *Project Rewire*, making it a must-read for anyone who cares about the health of our democracy.

—*Allison Hantschel*
[Athenae of *First Draft*]

PREFACE

ONCE UPON A TIME, the news business was my passion. It consumed me—my time, my energy, my ambitions, my waking moments. For nearly 25 years, all that mattered to me, aside from my family, was my work as a journalist, writing stories, informing the people, keeping an eye on public servants, holding government accountable. Like a lot of people in those days, I went into journalism because I thought I could make a difference in the world.

Then one day, I walked away. Just like that, I quit. Cold turkey. After spending most of my adult life at a keyboard pounding out stories about car accidents, education issues, athletic events, state government, and especially, politics, I signed off my computer, got up from my desk, walked out the office door, and never looked back.

How does one kick a 25-year habit? Or more importantly, why?

The answer is simple: It just was not fun any more. The years that I was in the news business—from 1973 to 1997—spanned many of the years covered in this book. My personal experience as a journalist colors my view of what was happening in the field at large over the last quarter of the twentieth century. I think my experience is typical. By the late 1990s, journalism standards were eroding from their Watergate high. Editors wanted "light" stories, briefer pieces, and simplified fare—and that eliminated just about anything having to do with government or the important public policy issues of the day.

Well into middle age, I took stock of my preferences and abilities. I enjoyed reading and writing about serious issues and looked for a career that would allow me to do that. I settled on history. By taking a night class and studying on the weekends, I prepared for the graduate record exam and began the application process for graduate school. Two weeks before the semester started at the University of Michigan, I went on vacation and told my editor I would not be coming back.

Now, with a doctorate in history and as a part-time lecturer at the University of Michigan, I consider myself a historian, not a journalist. Yet I remain a news consumer. I care about the news and still think good reporting matters. When *MoveOn.org* asked for volunteers for a media corps to hold journalists and news-gathering organizations accountable, I signed on. And in 2004, when *MoveOn.org* solicited its media corps members for people to help Robert Greenwald research a movie on Fox News Channel, I volunteered again. Watching the blatant bias on Fox News opened my eyes to how low journalism had sunk.

After the premier of Greenwald's *Outfoxed: Rupert Murdoch's War on Journalism,* eight of us researchers established a blog called *News Hounds* with the aid of Greenwald's producer, Jim Gilliam, and continued our Fox-watching. Now there are nine of us—ChrisH, Deb, Donna, Ellen, Janie, Marie Therese, Melanie, Nancy, and me. We are part of an Internet media watch-dog phenomenon that I believe holds great promise for prodding journalism to reform itself.

With its single-minded emphasis on Fox News, the *News Hounds* blog is not the place to discuss the field of journalism as a whole. Tom Sumner's Informed Citizen Series seemed the ideal place to lay out what happened to the news business and to let some of the best writers on the Internet analyze and interpret it.

Thus, as a history of journalism, *Project Rewire* is a synthesis of my three careers—journalist, historian, blogger. Perhaps because of the continuing work of the bloggers reprinted in *Project Rewire*, a historian 25 years from now will write the next installment. As a blogger, I'm optimistic that it will have a happier ending.

—J.D

UNWIRED:
how the media got disconnected

by Judy Daubenmier

THE ERA WAS A LOT LIKE THIS ONE. America's leaders felt the country was under attack from unseen enemies both inside and outside the nation's borders. Be wary of people acting differently, they said. The American way of life was in danger, they said. Survival was at stake, they said. We were at war, they said. A "cold" war, not a "shooting" war, but a war, they said.

Most people believed it, for a while. Most Americans believed that godless communists were undermining American values—in Hollywood, universities, and the State Department—and acquiesced to a campaign of intimidation and investigation orchestrated by politicians wielding the shadow of innuendo like the sword of truth.

The worst was Senator Joseph McCarthy. He met his match when a serious journalist put a new communications medium to the task of exposing McCarthy as a zealot who used unfounded accusations to bully innocent people for the sake of building his own political career. Edward R. Murrow, backed by CBS News, helped bring McCarthy down by investigating the investigator and revealing the results on television.

Yet within a few years, the CBS newsman told an audience in Chicago that the very medium he had used to humble Joe McCarthy was being used "to insulate the citizenry from the hard and demanding realities which must be faced if we are to survive." The powerful communications tool of television, he warned, was in danger of being reduced to "wires and lights in a box."[1]

If Murrow could issue such a warning during the era often called the Golden Age of Television, what would he say about the state of the medium in the early twenty-first century? What would the famed World War II correspondent say about journalists acting as cheerleaders for the Bush administration's rush to war in Iraq, about embedded war correspondents, about networks devoted to pushing the talking points of a particular political party?

There is no way of knowing for sure, but besides saying, "I told you so," Murrow may have wanted to know how it happened so fast. One way to answer that question is to look to the pioneers in a medium as young as television was when Murrow made his mark on it—writers in the progressive blogosphere who excel in a medium that also depends on wires and lights in a box but moves faster, has more transparency, and is more democratic than the one in which Murrow pioneered. Standing outside the mainstream media, writers for the Internet have been freer to criticize and, occasionally, praise journalists for newspapers, magazines, radio, network television, and cable channels than even Murrow was. Their musings on the state of contemporary news gathering and editorializing paint a mostly gloomy picture of the accomplishments and character of Murrow's successors. Yet a few progressive bloggers and Internet journalists say there may yet be time for contemporary journalism to save itself—and they urge quick action, believing, as Murrow did, that in many ways the nation's survival depends on exposing the public to reality rather than insulting it from it.

In that regard, bloggers are in good company. None other than Thomas Jefferson underscored the value of free and independent journalists to the nation. "Were it left for me to decide whether we should have a government without newspapers, or newspapers without a government, I should not hesitate a moment to prefer the latter," he said. Bloggers did not exist when Jefferson made that statement. Neither did White House spokespeople, government-issued propaganda masquerading as news, or journalists secretly on the government payroll. The last three developments blur the line between government and an independent press. Perhaps progressive bloggers that aggressively critique and occasionally compete with the mainstream media will save us from a captive press by being for the press what the press is supposed to be for government—a watchdog that is vigilant, vigorous, and vociferous.

Jefferson rightly observed that a free press was vital to our civic dialogue, from pre-revolutionary days to the present. Tom Paine's pamphlet *Common Sense*, for example, planted the seed for independence from Great Britain, as opposed to a mere tax protest, throughout the colonies. Later, James Madison, Alexander Hamilton, and John Jay argued the case for ratification of the proposed constitution for the new republic through articles they wrote collectively, called the Federalist Papers. In the antebellum U.S., the abolitionist press kept up a steady drumbeat of condemnation of slavery by printing slave autobiographies that put a human face on the cruelty of the institution. Harriet Beecher Stowe's publication of *Uncle Tom's Cabin* was pivotal in turning the nation's heart away from slavery. From 1851–1852, Stowe's work was published as a serial by the anti-slavery publication *The National Era*.

While the nation's newspapers were partisan publications throughout the nineteenth century, by the twentieth century a code of objectivity had evolved. Newspapers ceased being organs for a political party and became independent of party although their ownership and status as profit-making businesses generally made them upholders of the status quo in society.

Newspapers occupied without challenge the position of Americans' premier source for information about current events until the tense days of the 1930s prior to the outbreak of World War II. A new communications medium, radio, needed material to furnish its listeners, and Columbia Broadcasting System sent Edward R. Murrow, then 27, to Europe in 1937 to line up speakers for the network. He was originally called "the director of talks," but he soon transformed that role.

Murrow pioneered the role of broadcast journalist—a journalist who would witness events and report that information to the world orally over the radio rather than in newsprint. When war broke out in Europe, Murrow broadcast from the rooftops of London, reporting on Germany's invasion of Poland, the courage of Londoners during the blitz, the terror of a bombing run over Germany, and the horror of the Holocaust. The sound of Murrow's voice and his trademark phrase, "This is London," opening his broadcasts became familiar to millions of Americans.[2]

After the war, Murrow reluctantly moved into the rapidly growing field of television news. His radio show, *Hear It Now*, became *See It Now* on CBS Television. Although Murrow's show was popular, his decision to challenge the red scare tactics of Senator Joseph McCarthy, R-Wisconsin, eventually strained his relations with CBS. Murrow had noticed a *Detroit News* article about a Dexter, Michigan, man who was dismissed from the reserves of the Army Air Corps after being classified as a poor security risk. The man, Milo Radulovich, was fighting his dismissal, which was based on the fact that his immigrant father subscribed to two Serbian-language newspapers—one communist and one anti-communist—to keep up with Serbian news.[3]

CBS producer Fred Friendly backed Murrow and sent a reporter to Dexter, Michigan, to interview Radulovich for *See It Now*. Network executives, however, were so nervous about a story challenging the federal government and seeming to take the side of a potential subversive during the Cold War that they refused to advertise the segment. Furthermore, the sponsor of *See It Now*, Alcoa Aluminum, canceled its ad for the show because it was afraid of losing contracts with the Air Force. Friendly and Murrow were undaunted, however, and promoted the show with their own money, buying an ad in *The New York Times* in advance of the program. In the end, Friendly and Murrow's instincts were correct, as was Murrow's reporting. The public response to the show was overwhelmingly favorable. And five weeks later, Secretary of the Air Force Harold E. Talbott cleared Radulovich of all charges and reinstated him in the service.[4]

After learning that McCarthy was preparing to attack him, Murrow took on the senator directly. Relying on material about McCarthy that Murrow had been collecting for years, the *See It Now* show of March 9, 1954, used the senator's own words and pictures to portray him as an out-of-control zealot wielding power recklessly over innocent Americans. Murrow gave McCarthy a chance to respond, but instead of rebutting the facts, the senator used the time to attack Murrow as "the leader of the jackal pack." The program began McCarthy's slide into disgrace. Rather than seeing the episode as a triumph, however, CBS canceled *See It Now*.[5]

While Murrow's news magazine did not survive the era, the 1950s saw television news come into its own in other ways. Newscasts expanded from fifteen minutes to thirty. Equipment became smaller, lighter, and more portable. More and more Americans had televisions in their living rooms. And there was a compelling story to cover—the modern civil rights movement. Beginning in the mid-1950s with the Montgomery Bus Boycott of 1955, television moved out of the studios and into the streets to cover the non-violent civil rights demonstrations of African-Americans in the South and the sometimes shockingly harsh reaction of southern law enforcement authorities. The Museum of Broadcast Communications lists as "among the most enduring images" broadcast from the period shots of empty buses from the Montgomery bus boycott, white mobs surrounding black students escorted to Ole Miss by federal troops, the voting rights march in Selma, Alabama, and black demonstrators, including many children, being swept down the street by water rushing from fire hydrants turned on by city officials. "Unquestionably, this was compelling and revolutionary television," wrote Anna Everett in an article on the civil rights movement and television.[6]

Television inserted itself into American politics in 1960, when Democrat John Kennedy and Republican Richard Nixon participated in four televised debates during their campaign for president. More than 70 million Americans watched the first debate, in which the smooth, fit-looking Kennedy presented such a contrast to Nixon, wearing an ill-fitting suit and showing a five o'clock shadow. The chance to see both men in action no doubt influenced television viewers to consider Kennedy the victor, while those who heard the debate on radio thought Nixon had won. Although the debates were not a turning point in the campaign, the encounters did help Kennedy solidify his support among Democrats. The debates also set a precedent for other campaigns, both in the U.S. and around the world. Nixon refused to debate in 1968 and 1972, but since 1976 debates have been a fixture in American presidential campaigns. Federal law requires presidential candidates who accept federal campaign funds to participate in debates.[7]

As television increasingly became a part of the nation's political dialogue throughout the 1960s and 1970s, newspapers remained a significant force in the nation's civic life. Television had shown itself superior at dramatizing events and spreading information to a broader public, but newspaper coverage often provided the spark that drew television to cover events. Murrow, after all, had learned of the Radulovich case through a story in a Detroit newspaper, not through his own reporting. The print medium, as it would soon become known, remained superior at covering complex stories that did not lend themselves to visual images and to stories that required patient probing for information and sources—investigative reporting. Newspapers, in fact, were crucial to two scandals that characterized the Nixon administration—the leaking of the Pentagon Papers and the unraveling of the tangle of Nixon administration corruption and abuse of power centered on the Watergate burglary.

The New York Times' decision to publish the Pentagon's secret history of the Vietnam War, known as the Pentagon Papers, precipitated one of the most important court cases involving freedom of the press in U.S. history. Leaked to 19 newspapers by Daniel Ellsberg, a former Pentagon official and analyst for The Rand Corporation, the Pentagon Papers revealed the decision-making process behind the U.S. decision to increase its participation in Vietnam. After *The Times* published the first installment on June 13, 1971, the Nixon Administration went to court to halt publication of more of the papers on the grounds of protecting national security. The administration won an injunction barring the *Times*, and also the *Washington Post,* from publishing more of the material from the documents. On June 30, 1971, the U.S. Supreme Court decided 6–3 to lift the publication ban and cleared the way for the newspapers to resume publishing the Pentagon Papers. Significantly, it was newspapers to whom Ellsberg leaked the documents and it was newspapers that put their reputations and resources on the line in the face of government attempts at censorship.[8] Not only was the story itself more suited to newspapers than television because of the newspapers' ability to reproduce the documents in a form easily accessible for the public; but, with a pedigree in news gathering much longer than that of television news programs, newspapers also had more experience in government challenges to their right to publish—more than two hundred years of experience, in fact. (After all, the foundational case establishing freedom of the press in the United States involved a clash between a British colonial governor and a critical New York newspaper publisher named John Peter Zenger.[9]) The federal government later prosecuted Ellsberg for leaking the papers, but the 12 felony counts against him were dismissed in 1973 because of government misconduct in the case, including a break-in at the office of Ellsberg's psychiatrist.[10]

Newspapers again were at the forefront in uncovering the Nixon administration's connections to the burglary of Democratic National Committee headquarters in the Watergate office complex in June 1972. The five burglars and two former White House aides all pleaded guilty to various charges in connection with the act, but unbeknownst to the public, they had been receiving hush money, with Nixon's knowledge. Through painstaking and relentless reporting, a pair of *Washington Post* reporters, Bob Woodward and Carl Bernstein, succeeded in linking the Watergate burglars to the White House. Without their pursuit of the story, the public knowledge of Watergate burglary might have remained nothing more than the "third-rate burglary" that Nixon spokesman Ron Ziegler called it. Instead, the reporting of Woodward and Bernstein helped create the momentum for further investigations, including appointment of a special prosecution, hearings before the Senate Watergate committee, and a House Judiciary Committee preparation for impeachment proceedings.[11]

Television networks broadcast the important hearings which made the faces of H.R. Haldleman, John Ehrlichman, John Dean, and Senator Sam Ervin familiar to millions of Americans. Such coverage brought the issue home to American voters, demonstrated the importance of the issues in dispute, and helped sustain the momentum of the congressional hearings. Yet the visual media's role in exposing the scandal had been limited. Therein lies the paradox of the bifurcated impact of the American news media. Television's influence on the news was expanding, but it was not necessarily replacing the influence of newspapers. By 1969, television had become a significant source of news for Americans. The three networks' nightly news programs had a combined 50 percent rating, meaning half of all the television sets in the country were tuned to one of the three network news shows. The nightly news shows had an 85 percent share, meaning 85 percent of all the TV sets in use were tuned to one of the networks.[12] Despite the growing reach of television news, however, the networks did not routinely perform the government watchdog role that newspapers historically carried out. While Murrow and CBS had done the investigations of McCarthy in the 1950s, the investigations uncovering the potential significance of the Watergate burglary 20 years later were paid for by newspapers, not television networks. Television extended the reach of those stories and covered them in different ways that provided an immediacy and drama to the events of the day. Television, for example, provided a valuable service in its coverage of the Vietnam War—furnishing timely, sustained coverage of a conflict half a world away, the first war brought to Americans' homes in living color. Beginning in the 1960s, network news programs became the target of a conservative critique aimed at muzzling their voices. Beginning with the days of the Vietnam War and Watergate, conservatives have kept up a vigorous attack against the news operations of the three major networks as liberal. The right wing began vilifying veteran CBS News anchor Walter Cronkite after his 1968 editorial urging U.S. withdrawal from South Vietnam and the opening of negotiations with the North. Beginning in 1969, Accuracy in Media (AIM), with support from the deep pockets of the oil and banking fortune of conservative Richard Mellon Scaife, has beaten the drum of media liberalism.

Soon, another factor would help speed television news' retreat from investigative journalism—the advent of consultants in the 1970s paid to increase the ratings of television news programs. Consultants such as Frank Magid and Associates, Audience Research and Development, McHugh-Hoffman, Broadcast Image Group, and others, perform audience research, helping shape the news delivered to what audience surveys show viewers think they want. A sample of the advice dispensed was this suggestion to a woman reporter about the possibility of covering a tragedy such as the Oklahoma City bombing: "You have to ask yourself: If there was a terrible tragedy in my area and that footage went all around the country—which could very well happen—would you be embarrassed? Would you be ashamed? Would you say to yourself, Oh, my God, I wore the wrong thing that day?" Besides such "dress for tragedy" tips, the consultants help skew television news toward concern with image, "soft" news, graphics, chit-chat among anchors, shorter stories—all trends that move television away from hard-hitting stories related to government, politics, and world affairs.[13]

In 1985, media critic Neil Postman warned that because of television, Americans were in danger of "amusing ourselves to death." In his book by that name, Postman warned that television was transforming everything into entertainment or show business.[14] One measure of that is the proportion of fluff topics that make up the nightly newscasts on broadcast television. Between 1977 and June of 2001, the percent of stories related to celebrities, entertainment, and lifestyle topics rose from 6 percent of the total to 18 percent. Meanwhile, the percentage of stories related to government plunged from 37 percent in 1977 to 5 percent in June 2001. The disaster of 2001 began a slow reversal of those trends, so that by 2004, celebrity, entertainment, and lifestyle stories amounted to 7 percent of the total, while government coverage was back up to 27 percent.[15]

This "dumbing down" of the news has brought with it an emphasis on certain types of stories—the disappearance of young, white females such as Natalee Holloway, the trial of celebrities such as Michael Jackson, and so on. Arianna Huffington counted how many news segments mentioned either Holloway or Jackson during an eight-week period in 2005 and compared that to the number that mentioned the "Downing Street Memo," a memo from the British government that discussed Bush administration policy and U.S. intelligence prior to the war in Iraq. The totals—for six broadcast and cable channels—were 56 segments on the Downing Street Memo, 646 segments for Natalee Holloway, and 1,490 for Jackson's trial. While news executives claim news on Holloway and Jackson are what people who watch these stations want, Huffington maintains that tens of millions of people are not watching any of these channels and must want something else, adding, "there are huge slices of audience a real news operation could go after."[16]

With television increasingly cowed by the right wing and content with its new "happy talk" formats, newspapers remained the logical source of watchdog journalism, but their ability to finance such projects depended on circulation, which was under pressure from television news. Newspapers held their own against television until 1970, when they were on the verge of a downward slide in circulation that would make it harder for them to pay for such investigative projects. The percentage of Americans reading newspapers began to drop much earlier—in the late 1940s—but the problem was masked by growth in the U.S. population, which kept circulation rising until 1970. At that point, newspaper circulation flattened out until 1990, when it began to actually decline. Between 1990 and 2002, circulation dropped at the rate of 1 percent every year. By 2002, 55 million newspapers were sold daily, compared to the 1970 peak of 62 million. Newspaper readership, as opposed to newspaper sales, also was declining rapidly. In 2004, 60 percent of Americans surveyed by the Pew Research Center said they read a newspaper regularly, down 15 percentage points since the peak of 75 percent in 1992 and the lowest since Pew began the survey in 1990.[17]

The 1990s were a watershed for television news as well. The three networks had had competition from CNN beginning in 1980, but even with AIM's carping, millions of Americans still felt comfortable with hearing the news of the world every evening from one of the anchors of the Big Three networks: ABC's Peter Jennings, CBS's Dan Rather, or NBC's Tom Brokaw. Although none of them ever earned the unofficial title of "most trusted man in America" that many viewers conferred on CBS's Walter Cronkite, the trio of big anchors challenged each other but went unchallenged as a group from the mid-1980s through the mid-1990s. In times of crisis, most Americans turned to them for breaking news, explanations, behind-the-scene interviews, and in-depth analysis. The big anchors held Americans' hands during disasters, such as the 1986 Challenger shuttle disaster, or the September 11 attacks on the World Trade Center towers and the Pentagon. During such times, the anchors knit together the scraps of information from official sources, reporters in the field, and their own observations to try to make sense of unfolding events.

At times, each was subject to criticism, often from the right, for being too tough on the nation's leaders. Jennings defended himself, for example, from charges that he was soft on the war on Iraq, saying, "This role is designed to question the behavior of government officials on behalf of the public."[18] Tom Brokaw viewed his job in part as an obligation to direct "the bright light of journalistic sunshine" on the wrongs in society, prompting some people to charge bias. "Look, I've been dealing with this myself since the Vietnam War and the civil rights movement, when reporters were accused of having a liberal bias. The fact of the matter is, if I don't establish a bond with the NBC News audience that is based on my credibility and my integrity, then I go out of business. We've been doing this for a long time. *NBC Nightly News* still has the largest single audience of any media outlet, print and electronic, in the news business. The simple test is that if people thought I had a bias, they wouldn't watch me," he said.[19] Rather described his job—the job of any reporter—as that of trying to be "an honest broker of information" who is willing to ask tough questions, remains skeptical of those in power and tries to be accurate and fair, while admitting no one can do that 100 percent of the time. "The core of the practice of journalism has to be integrity," he said.[20]

Mid-way through the reign of the Big Three, the American media landscape changed in fundamental ways. AIM's single-pronged attack on American media would have been of little effect had the Federal Communications Commission not dropped its rules requiring broadcasters to provide balanced programming. The fairness doctrine, as it was called, required equal time for opposing points of view in the programming of broadcast stations. The FCC based the doctrine on the philosophy that a broadcasting license was a public trust and its holder owed a duty to the public to provide balanced discussion of important issues. Broadcast journalists complained that the balancing requirement unduly constrained their First Amendment freedoms and kept them from reporting on controversial topics. Furthermore, during Ronald Reagan's administration, the philosophy of deregulating all government-regulated industries and allowing the rules of the marketplace to function ruled in Washington. In 1987, the FCC stopped enforcing the fairness doctrine. Federal courts upheld the commission's decision.

The disappearance of the fairness doctrine opened the airwaves to a flood of new programming—political commentary, especially right-wing political commentary. In 1988, Rush Limbaugh took his flamboyant AM radio talk show into national syndication through media giant Clear Channel Communications. Freed from the responsibility of presenting a range of viewpoints, broadcast stations aired Limbaugh's attacks on liberals and the "liberal media" without opportunity for rebuttal. The formula for conservative talk radio consisted of vigorous attacks that demonized liberal politicians and liberal ideas and undermined the credibility of mainstream media by labeling them liberal as well. Limbaugh indoctrinated his listeners with the belief that only he told the unvarnished truth and the media (of which he, in somewhat of a contradiction, denied being a part) was biased. Limbaugh's attacks were designed to induce outrage in his listeners, to advance a conservative agenda, and to drive liberal ideas underground.

Limbaugh's success bred a flock of imitators—G. Gordon Liddy, Bill O'Reilly, Sean Hannity, Oliver North, Michael Savage, Armstrong Williams, Laura Ingraham, and so on. By 2004, conservatives dominated political talk radio—by a ratio of more than ten hours for right-wing commentary to just three for progressive discussion. A survey by Democracy Radio of 691 radio stations in the top 120 radio markets found 149 local conservative programs being broadcast for 2,349 hours a week, compared to 49 local progressive programs broadcast for a total of 555 weekly broadcast hours. Those stations also broadcast 19 national conservative programs which, including airing by 3,394 affiliates, totaled 39,382 hours each week. The stations also broadcast 19 national progressive programs, but with just 250 affiliates, the broadcast hours each week came to 2,487. Total conservative programming amounted to 41,731 hours each week, to just 3,042 hours for progressive commentary.[21]

In 1996, Rupert Murdoch brought the Republican agenda to television with the premier of his cable news channel, Fox News. Former Republican campaign strategist Roger Ailes headed the network and set it on an editorial course that deliberately favored the right wing while simultaneously proclaiming itself as "fair and balanced." Fox News favored displays of the American flag, flashy graphics, white anchors and reporters, and conservative pundits. While its chief rival, CNN, stressed breaking news reported from its bureaus around the world, Fox News stressed a stable of hired experts giving their opinions on news events—opinions that miraculously mirrored those of the Republican Party.

Even as they ranted against a media supposedly biased against them, top Republicans admitted it was the political equivalent of "working the refs" in sports. In one breath, former Republican Party Chair Rich Bond could complain during the 1992 presidential campaign that, "I think we know who the media want to win this election—and I don't think it's George Bush." In the next breath, Bond could admit, "There is some strategy to it [bashing the 'liberal' media]. . . . If you watch any great coach, what they try to do is 'work the refs.' Maybe the ref will

cut you a little slack on the next one."[22] Nevertheless, such
two-faced talk began to have an effect on the public views of
the media and of the actions of the news media.

A study published in Communications Research in 1999
found that the percentage of Americans who described the
media as biased in favor of liberals more than doubled between
1988 and 1996—rising from 12 percent in 1988 to 43 percent
in 1996. The authors of the study found that the increase occurred even as they found virtually no change in actual pro-
liberal or anti-conservative bias in reporting on the presidential
candidates. Instead, the authors said claims by conservatives,
especially candidates, drove the increase in public perception
of the media as biased toward liberals, as did the media's coverage of its alleged liberal bias. As Republican candidates and
their supporters, such as right-wing radio figures, alleged an
industry-wide liberal media bias, "journalists have little choice
but to report these charges to demonstrate that they are not
biased," the study said. Liberal candidates, on the other hand,
rarely complained of a conservative bias in the news media so
that conservative complaints were allowed to dominate the discourse. The authors conclude that citizens now prefer to have
political elites, such as candidates and party officials, keeping
watch over the media, "which would be an ironic reversal of
the democratic ideal of citizens relying on news media to monitor elites."[23]

The unrelenting attacks on the mainstream media as biased
and liberal began taking a toll on its objectivity. The 2000 presidential campaign was a watershed in terms of liberal views of
the mainstream media. Increasingly, liberals began to see the
mainstream media as consciously conservative, rather than
making an attempt to be objective. The mainstream media's

nitpicking coverage of Vice President Al Gore's campaign defied any attempt to label the media as biased in favor of liberals. A study by the Pew Research Center and the Project for Excellence in Journalism documented media bias against Gore even before the election. More than three-fourths of the 2,400 newspaper, television and Internet stories examined either claimed that Gore habitually lied or exaggerated, or that he was tainted by scandal. In an article for *Columbia Journalism Review*, Jane Hall said her own review of more than a hundred news stories, as well as cable and network television shows, found the same sort of negative coverage of Gore. "The substance of what Gore has been saying in speeches around the country often has been wrapped in reporters' cynical language that effectively casts doubt about his motives before he even opens his mouth," Hall wrote. Hall suggested that reporters found George Bush more likeable as a person and that their coverage reflected his back-slapping ways with members of the media.[24]

Even conservatives commented on the treatment so-called objective news reporters dished out to Gore. Joe Scarborough, a former Republican congressman turned right-wing MSNBC-talk-show-host, said in an appearance on MSNBC's *Hardball*, that during the 2000 election, reporters "were fairly brutal to Al Gore. I think they hit him hard on a lot of things like inventing the Internet and some of those other things, and I think there was a generalization they bought into that, if they had done that to a Republican candidate, I'd be going on your show saying, you know, that they were being biased." Gore, of course, never made the statement that he invented the Internet. It had originated in a GOP fax and was picked up uncritically by news reporters.[25]

The media's performance on election night ultimately shredded any illusions liberals had of fairness in the mainstream media (although it did not affect the conservative claims of liberal bias). Among the major television networks, CBS initially called Florida for Al Gore, then retracted it. Ignoring a dwindling Bush lead in Florida as the night wore on, CBS awarded Florida to Bush immediately after Fox News did so, declaring Bush president-elect. NBC and ABC also put Florida in Bush's column after Fox News declared it for Bush. And who made the call at Fox News? George Bush's cousin, John Ellis. Ellis admitted talking to Bush five times on election night, but denied giving his relative any confidential voter exit polling data.[26] In testimony prepared for a congressional inquiry into the networks' election night performance, Fox News Chairman and CEO Roger Ailes assured the House Energy and Commerce Committee that, "Through our self-examination and investigation we have determined that there was no intentional political favoritism in play on election night on the part of Fox News."[27] As other commentators were quick to point out, however, the effect of Fox News' call was politically favorable to Bush. "The other networks quickly followed suit. The call was retracted hours later, but not until long after it had registered its impact: For the next 35 tortuous days, Bush was the presumed president-elect, and Al Gore the presumed sore loser," wrote Rob Garver.[28] Had the networks simply reported the truth—that the race was too close to call and the winner was unknown—the pro-Bush U.S. Supreme Court might have been more cautious about ending the vote recount in Florida.

The pull that Fox News exerted on the other networks on Election Night 2000 demonstrated what Jeff Cohen called the "Fox effect." Cohen, formerly senior producer for the Phil

Donahue Prime Time show on MSNBC, was interviewed about his experience for the film *Outfoxed: Rupert Murdoch's War on Journalism.* "From the beginning they were saying to us we have to be balanced. . . . Don't be too partisan. Don't be too angry. Now by the end of our tenure, balance wasn't enough. And this is the 'Fox Effect.' They mandated that any time we had, if we had two left-wing guests, we had to have three right-wing guests. If we had one anti-war guest, we had to have two pro-war guests. And that's how we ended the show. So, we're trying to outfox Fox. You cannot outfox Fox. But MSNBC and the others have tried," Cohen said.[29]

Whether it was the Fox effect or something else, the media deserted their posts as government watchdog during the run-up to the invasion of Iraq. Reporters showed an amazing willingness to take President Bush at his word about the existence of Weapons of Mass Destruction and the need for regime change in Iraq. Even the conservatives' poster child for media liberal bias, CBS anchor Dan Rather, admitted putting patriotism before professional responsibility. Rather told a Harvard University forum on Iraq war coverage: "Look, when a president of the United States, any president, Republican or Democrat, says these are the facts, there is heavy prejudice, including my own, to give him the benefit of any doubt, and for that I do not apologize."[30]

Besides refusing to challenge the Republican administration, the media also refused to air the views of those sources who did disagree with the president's team. A study of sources interviewed on six television networks and television channels during the first three weeks of the Iraq War found that 64 percent favored the war, while only 10 percent were against it. Among guests who were from the U.S., 71 percent favored the war and just 3 percent opposed it. The study done by Fairness and Accuracy in Reporting covered ABC World News Tonight, CBS Evening News, NBC Nightly News, CNN's Wolf Blitzer Reports, Fox News' Special Report with Brit Hume, and PBS' NewsHour with Jim Lehrer. FAIR found little difference between the guests of Fox News and CBS. Of the sources interviewed by Fox News, 81 percent were pro-war; the figure for CBS was 77 percent.[31]

Far from the safety of the studios, the embedding of reporters with combat units guaranteed more uncritical coverage of the war, delivered only from the vantage point of those doing the shooting. Journalists dependant on the troops for food, water, protection, and transportation were unlikely to file critical stories about what they saw. Some, however, committed even more grievous journalistic sins. Jules Crittenden, a reporter for the *Boston Herald*, admitted helping direct fire at three Iraqis for troops of the 3rd Infantry Division with which he was embedded. Crittenden offered no apologies for crossing the line from journalist to combatant, writing, "Now that I have assisted in the deaths of three human beings in the war I was sent to cover, I'm sure there are some people who will question my ethics, my objectivity, etc. I'll keep the arguments short. Screw them, they weren't there. But they are welcome to join me next time if they care to test their professionalism."[32]

Long after Bush declared the end of major combat operations in Iraq, some major American media decided to reconsider their roles in the push for war. A couple of factors prompted the need for the collective examination of conscience. For one, Bush's rationale for the war had unraveled. The American occupiers had found no sign of the stockpiles of Weapons of Mass Destruction which the Bush administration had warned about with its mushroom-cloud metaphors. Furthermore, the war dragged on without evidence of progress either of restoring the pre-invasion quality of life or quashing the insurgency. By May 2004, *The New York Times* apologized for its poor coverage prior to the war. Claiming that problems with its coverage were systemic rather than the fault of individual reporters, *The Times* said it found "a number of instances of coverage that was not as rigorous as it should have been. In some cases, information that was controversial then, and seems questionable now, was insufficiently qualified or allowed to stand unchallenged. Looking back, we wish we had been more aggressive in reexamining the claims as new evidence emerged—or failed to emerge."[33]

While the *Times* blamed institutional factors for the breakdown in its coverage, most of the reporting was done by veteran reporter Judith Miller, who relied on information supplied by Ahmad Chalabi despite the fact that much of the material he supplied had been questioned by the CIA.[34] Miller's reporting was controversial within the newspaper at the time but became even more so when she went to jail to protect her source in Treasongate, the investigation into whether someone within the Bush Administration leaked to the press the name of CIA operative Valerie Plame. The implication was that Miller was too cozy with members of the Bush administration, including I. Lewis (Scooter) Libbey, Vice President Dick Cheney's chief of staff and her source in the Plame affair.[35]

At the *Washington Post*, Executive Editor Leonard Downie, Jr. has taken responsibility for failing to more prominently display stories that questioned the administration's evidence on WMD and other aspects of its war motives and plans. Pentagon correspondent Thomas Ricks complained, "The paper was not front-paging stuff. Administration assertions were on the front page. Things that challenged the administration were on A18 on Sunday or A24 on Monday. There was an attitude among editors: Look, we're going to war, why do we even worry about all this contrary stuff?" Nearly seventeen months after the nation went to war, Downie agreed, "Not enough of those stories were put on the front page. That was a mistake on my part." He still doubted, however, whether better reporting and editing during the run-up to the war would have prevented the U.S. attack.[36]

Despite the second thoughts by news organizations such as *The New York Times* and the *Washington Post,* at least one well-known journalist stands by his work on the runup to the Iraq invasion and on the issue of Iraq's alleged possession of Weapons of Mass Destruction. Ted Koppel, host of ABC-TV's *Nightline* from its beginnings with the Iranian hostage crisis in 1979 through 2005, said he believed prior to the start of the war in March 2003 that Saddam Hussein had WMD and that members of the Bush administration believed it as well, but denied the press simply relied on the administration's assurances. "No, I don't just take their word for it. But when they tell me why they're going to war, I certainly have to give proper deference to . . . if the president says I'm going to war for reasons A, B and C, I can't very well stand there and say, 'The president is not telling you the truth, the actual reason that he's going to war is some reason he hasn't even mentioned.' I as a reporter at least have to say, 'Here's what the president is saying. Here's what the secretary of defense is saying. Here's what the director of the CIA is saying. Here's what the members of Congress are saying.' And indeed, when everyone at that point who has access to the classified information is with more or less one voice agreeing that, yes, there appears to be evidence that Saddam Hussein still has weapons of mass destruction—maybe not nuclear, but certainly chemical and probably biological—are you suggesting that the entire American press corps then say, 'Well, horse manure.'"[37] Koppel contended he had no way of checking what Bush was saying.

Other journalists reflecting on the media's performance prior to the Iraq invasion cited professional constraints as a hindrance to hard-hitting reporting. The professional obligation to be balanced in reporting, the press of deadlines, and the speed with which developments occur all conspire to muddy many punches reporters try to deliver. "One of the real challenges, I think, in daily journalism, is it's easy to have the appearance of balance; you know, 'Bush charged that Kerry was a serial murderer, Kerry denied it.' So there both sides have had their say, so it's balanced, and it's harder to really do a substantive analysis of charge and counter-charge, especially if it turns out that one side is right and the other is wrong," said Susan Page of *USA Today* in a forum on journalism. "You can't just say the president is lying," agreed Elizabeth Bumiller of *The New York Times*.[38]

Other news organizations, however, did find a way to cast doubt on administration claims without resorting to playground-style name-calling. In February 2003, shortly after U.S. Secretary of State Colin Powell made his dramatic case to the United Nations about Iraq weapons, members of Ansar al-Islam invited Western journalists to visit a site in Kurdish-held northern Iraq that Powell had named as a chemical weapons production site. BBC Television broadcast a report from the site, which consisted of some buildings previously used as radio and TV studios. "At the back of a row of buildings there was one drum which had originally contained plastic-related chemicals but it was empty. The Ansar said it had been used to store fuel. If the site had been used for producing or experimenting in chemical or biological weapons, there was no obvious sign that that is still the case," reported BBC correspondent Jim Muir. Muir's report was carefully hedged, including references to the Ansar's motives for showing journalists the site (a desire to avoid being attacked). Yet it gave viewers the idea that problems existed with Powell's evidence, without ever saying "horse manure."[39]

It was not professional constraints, but a seeming lack of them, that contributed to a series of embarrassing mistakes by the nation's high-profile media. Jayson Blair resigned as a reporter for *The New York Times* in May 2003 after the newspaper's editors discovered he had stolen information from stories from other newspapers or fabricated it in 36 of 73 articles written in a seven-month span.[40] CBS News' highly respected "60 Minutes Wednesday" was embarrassed when questions were raised by right-wing bloggers about the authenticity of memos used in a story regarding George Bush's service in the Texas National Guard. After 12 days of defending the accuracy of the story, which ran during the 2004 election campaign, the network appointed an independent panel to look into the circumstances surrounding the production of the story. The panel stopped short of calling the memos forgeries, only concluding that there were serious questions about their authenticity, but it did fault the story's producers for rushing the story on the air without proper vetting and for believing too zealously in the truth of the story. CBS News anchor Dan Rather, long a target of the right-wing, announced in the midst of the investigation that he was retiring. The network also asked three executives to resign and fired a fourth. Their departures did not calm the right-wing storm over the matter. Rush Limbaugh, for example, took the incident as evidence that CBS "had an axe to grind" with Bush.[41]

In May 2005, *Newsweek* magazine took its turn on the hot seat for a story which said that interrogators at the prison at Guantanamo Bay had flushed a copy of the Koran down the toilet. After the story was translated into Arabic and picked up by news outlets in the Middle East, anti-American riots in which 15 people died broke out in Afghanistan, Pakistan, and other countries. Meanwhile, the anonymous source for the story had backed off the assertion that the incident was contained in a Pentagon report. *Newsweek* editors apologized for the story and said it was an honest mistake.[42]

While these incidents fed red meat to the right-wing attack dogs, these media critics had little to say when Fox News chief campaign reporter was caught ridiculing the man he was supposed to be covering. In October 2004, Carl Cameron posted on the channel's web site a story ridiculing Democratic presidential candidate John Kerry as a "metrosexual" who gets manicures. The network "reprimanded" Cameron, but allowed him to continue covering Kerry after taking a few days off.[43] AIM Editor Cliff Kincaid dismissed Cameron's false story as "peanuts" compared to blunders by the "liberal media."[44]

While these blunders generated a lot of heat, they deflected attention from more serious problems within the news business—especially pressure to make a profit exerted by corporate owners. Newspapers and television stations always have been in business to make money, but pressure to make money intensified once ownership became consolidated in a few large corporations. In 1996, the Republican-led Congress and President Clinton rewrote the federal telecommunications law in a way that favored big media companies. Restrictions on ownership of stations were loosened so that a single owner could control stations representing 35 percent of the national television market, up from 25 percent, while restrictions on the number of radio stations owned by one entity were lifted entirely.

The 2004 version of the annual State of the News Media report laid out the picture on ownership for all media: 22 companies own newspapers with 70 percent of the nation's daily circulation; the top 20 companies operate more than 20 percent of all radio stations in the country, with Clear Channel operating stations in 191 of the 289 Arbitron-rated markets; just 10 companies own 30 percent of all local television stations, reaching 85 percent of all the nation's television households, and the national television networks are owned by giant corporations for whom television news, in particular, is a miniscule part of their operations.[45]

Such concentration of ownership has myriad effects—reduced diversity in viewpoints, standardized or "cookie-cutter" formats for local television news, more canned programming for radio, and so on. In theory, bigness should have given news organizations the resources to finance better news gathering practices—more bureaus around the world, more investigative reporters to pursue in-depth projects, and so on. Journalists reported that exactly the opposite has happened.

A former foreign correspondent for CBS News published a book in 2005 criticizing news organizations for abdicating their responsibility to the public in the 1990s by cutting back on foreign coverage at the same time that al Qaeda was growing as a threat to the U.S. Tom Fenton, in *Bad News: The Decline of Reporting, the Business of News, and the Danger to Us All,* says news organizations thought the end of the Cold War was a good excuse to start saving money on foreign bureaus. Fenton records his frustration at CBS' refusal to pay for him to go to

Afghanistan to interview Osama bin Laden in 1997. That, however, was only one of numerous demoralizing decisions by the network: A story on schoolchildren in Sarajevo killed because a producer found the war there "very depressing," another story on bin Laden dropped because it had "too many foreign names," and so on.[46]

CBS commentator Andy Rooney told Fenton the problem with the media today is that the bean-counters have taken over. "Money has taken over news. It was always a factor, but never what it is now. I think it's that these people at the top are driven to make money. . . . [Les] Moonves, his only desire is to keep the price of the stock up, to make more money for himself," Rooney told Fenton.[47] The result, according to Fenton, is that foreign news bureaus do little actual reporting themselves. Mostly, they repackage pictures with facts gathered by other news agencies. "Call it the news media's version of outsourcing . . . Don't shoot it, don't report it—just wrap it up and slap the CBS eye on it," he said.[48]

Fenton's views of the impact of bottom-line journalism are widely shared by his colleagues. A survey of 500 journalists by the Pew Research Center for the People and the Press found 66 percent of journalists for national media believe the drive to make money is hurting the profession, up from 41 percent in 1995. It also found that 45 percent of journalists believe that news reports are "full of factual errors," up from 30 percent in 1995. And 51 percent of journalists at national media believe the profession is going in the wrong direction. More than half of them also responded that the news media avoid complex issues, is too timid and has not been critical enough of President Bush.[49]

Not all the blame for the media's shirking of its responsibility can be laid at the door of corporate owners. Journalists themselves are supposed to bring idealism, a passion for the news, and insatiable curiosity to the job. In an age when a few journalists become famous and well-paid, some young people may be entering the field without that burning idealism. In Koppel's view, "Many people today want to get into journalism because they perceive it as a way to become famous and make a lot of money. It's not, of course. It really isn't. . . . You should get into journalism because you love it, because you can't believe that there is anything else in the world that is more exciting, more interesting, more fascinating. That's not necessarily the way things are today."[50]

For a short time in 2005, though, some reporters seemed to recover the zest for their craft that supposedly brought them to it in the first place. That moment came during coverage of Hurricane Katrina's devastation and the federal government's failure to even bring food and water to those stranded in New Orleans. As reporters struggled through the flooded streets of the city, they witnessed the misery of evacuees in the Super Dome and Convention Center and broadcast their pleas for help, even as members of the Bush Administration insisted everything possible was being done to rush in aid. The disjuncture jolted many journalists out of their usual willingness to grant credence to the official version of events. They began to more aggressively question the Bush Administration and to demand action. On *Nightline*, Ted Koppel took to task Michael Brown, then head of the Federal Emergency Management Agency. CNN's Anderson Cooper boldly asked one politician, "Do you get the anger that is out here?" Even on Fox News, Shepard Smith pestered a police officer, demanding to know when help would be coming for people left without water for days.[51]

In general, commentators on journalism praised the new

spirit of reporters and anchors as they sought to explain why it surfaced when it did. The BBC's Matt Wells opined that, "Amidst the horror, American broadcast journalism just might have grown its spine back, thanks to Katrina." Howard Kurtz of the *Washington Post* suggested reporters had rediscovered their sense of purpose. Others saw reporters as merely reflecting public outrage or regaining the aggressiveness of Watergate-era journalists. Jay Rosen explained the reinvigorated press as a shift in power away from the administration to journalists: The administration lost its ability to control the news agenda while at the same time, the versions of reality it offered were so blatantly wrong that reporters could easily rebut them without fear of contradiction. "Clueless federal officials seem to know less about what is happening than the journalists do, and sometimes less than an average TV viewer. This tips the balance of power toward the press, which is why we see such aggressive questioning and on-air criticism close to jeering," Rosen said. He was not optimistic about the power shift enduring for long, given that other situations government deals with are more abstract than the sight of bodies floating in flood waters and the smell of people living days without sanitation facilities. Rather than merely being tough or passionate, Rosen said, journalists need to think and let that thinking guide their reporting.[52]

Rosen's doubts about Katrina marking a tipping point in the balance of power between journalists and the Bush administration are doubly valid because the weakness of the news organizations as institutions occurs as the institution they are supposed to cover—government—gets better and better at shutting out journalistic scrutiny. The Bush administration avoids having the president do news conferences, punishes people who talk to reporters without authorization, and limits the president's public appearances to carefully scripted speeches in front of audiences guaranteed to be friendly, such as soldiers or business executives. Reporters have been pushed to the margins. Ron Suskind summed up the Bush media philosophy this way: "They view the press as another special interest in Washington, just like the prescription drug people. They say that they don't think it is good to offer lots of access and disclosure, to let people see what they do and why they do it, and to let anyone outside their inner circle know about the key debates that ultimately drive and precipitate policy. Essentially, the press is there to record their decisions."[53]

Ironically, competition within the news business makes it easier for the administration to manipulate reporters. With a wide range of television news shows on cable and broadcast television, Bush administration officials can choose which reporters will interview them. They can easily choose to appear on morning shows, where the interviewers are less well-versed in matters of national security than are reporters regularly covering the State Department or the Pentagon.[54] Even at news conferences, the president chooses which reporters will ask questions. With each reporter pursuing his or her own story, none is likely to help out the competition by asking a follow-up question to another reporter's tough query, even if one is asked.

While AIM and other right-wing groups continue to pressure the media to conform to their ideological bias, other groups are demanding more aggressive questioning of those in power. Bloggers and Internet journalists who cover the media are among the loudest voices begging journalists to show more courage in their reporting and urging networks and newspapers to embrace the Internet in creative ways as a mechanism for delivering their news products. Simultaneously, some groups are hoping to influence the rewrite of the 1996 Telecommunications Act in 2006 so that the consolidation of media into fewer and fewer hands is halted, or perhaps reversed. Independent media, financed by citizens, are springing up.

Yet in the end, thorough, hard-hitting reporting needs a sound financial basis that in the past has mostly been provided by the nation's newspapers. Although newspapers remain profitable in general, the outlook there is not good. Total readership of daily newspapers in the U.S. declined from 58.8 million in 1960 to 55.2 million in 2003, despite increases in the nation's population. The coming of age of television news, of course, drained newspapers' longtime dominance as the nation's news source during much of that time span. Short term trends, however, were equally discouraging—the percentage of adults reached by daily newspapers fell to 53.4 by the spring of 2004 from 58.8 in 1996.

For television news, the changes between 1996 and spring 2004 were even more disheartening. The percentage of American adults reached by television news programs fell to 38.2 percent from 45.3 percent. The reach of radio news programming dropped to 21.7 percent of U.S. adults by spring 2004 from 25.5 percent in 1996. Competition, which had allowed television to eat into newspapers' domination as a news source, also caused television's decline. Cable television news picked up the slack. By the spring of 2004, it reached 14.4 percent of the nation's adults, up from 11 percent in 1996.[55]

Even with the declines, newspapers and the major networks still reach larger audiences than the alternatives. In January 2006, the highest rated cable channel—Fox News Channel—averaged 1.6 million viewers. In contrast, the highest-rated network evening news program—NBC—averaged 10.15 million viewers.[56]

Is there a prescription for turning around this trend? Changing lifestyles may have made nightly newscasts less practical. With more two-career couples, fewer meals eaten at home, and parents shuttling children to after-school events, being home for a 6 p.m. newscast every night may simply be impossible for many adults. That may explain part of the shift to the always-available news of cable television. If so, network news should be able to exploit the Internet as an avenue for delivering its news product—stories that are better reported, more deeply sourced, and contain more context than what is usually available on cable.[57] ABC is already offering digital versions of its news, having launched *ABC News Now* in 2004 to provide news around the clock seven days a week. Internet users can be their own producers—constructing their own half-hour—or more—of news according to their own news, interests, and schedules.[58]

Newspapers also must learn to exploit the Internet. The range and depth of information they gather, package, and transmit—either on newsprint or electronically—on a daily basis remains unmatched by other sources. Although newspapers have Internet sites for disseminating their product, they have done little more than recycle what is in the newspapers rather than experimenting with adding video or audio or linking to other information. Such innovation seems essential if newspapers are to capture a larger share of younger people. Furthermore, revenue from those sites remains a small part of total newspaper earnings.[59]

Television networks would be well served by turning away from celebrity journalists, investing in more reporters, and re-opening foreign bureaus. CBS's *Evening News* program has seen

its ratings improve as it transisitions to a permanent replace-
ment for longtime anchor Dan Rather (network executives hired
Katie Couric from NBC's *Today Show* at a salary of $20 mil-
lion to read the evening news for CBS). Andy Rooney, the
crusty commentator on CBS's *60 Minutes*, opined that the
network should "take that $20 million, don't give it to Katie.
Give it to a bunch of reporters and make CBS news the best
news report in the world." Rooney recommended reopening
CBS bureaus in Warsaw and Buenos Aires. Networks might
even return to developing hour-long documentaries on current issues, such as the great 1960s exposés on hunger (*Hunger
in America*) and migrant workers (*Harvest of Shame*) that would
showcase in-depth work by its star (and not celebrity) reporters. To do such work, however, news executives need to free
their best reporters from the grind of day-to-day coverage and
allow them to follow leads, and especially their instincts. Covering routine White House bill-signings and press briefings
might even be de-emphasized as reporters separate themselves
from the pack being fed by administration flacks and go elsewhere to find news.[60]

Strengthening the bonds of trust between news organizations and the public should be an important priority for news
executives. That means rebuilding the wall that used to separate reporters (as opposed to talk show hosts or pundits) from
the people in the news. The wall has been breached routinely
in recent years. NBC reporter Maria Shriver, wife of Arnold
Schwarzenegger, actually contemplated continuing as a reporter
after her husband was elected governor of California. Andrea
Mitchell, also with NBC, kept her job as a reporter after wed-
ding Federal Reserve Board Chairman Alan Greenspan. And
Pete Williams went from being spokesman for the Pentagon in

George H.W. Bush's administration to reporting for NBC during the Clinton administration. The former aide to Vice President Dick Cheney has since gone on to cover the indictment of Cheney's chief of staff, I. Lewis (Scooter) Libby.[61] News organizations should demand that reporters avoid not only conflicts of interest, but also the appearance of conflicts of interest, as a way of underlining their independence.

Closely related is the need for news organization to correct the "Fox-ification" of their programming—the rightward tilt of guest selection as demonstrated by the FAIR report, as well as the dominance of conservative talk show hosts as compared to progressive ones. CNN, for example, added conservatives William Bennett, J.C. Watts, and Glenn Beck to its list of commentators without bulking up its stable of liberal commentators. Ideally, increased reporting would replace networks' reliance on such pundits as well.

Some of these changes may be spurred by competition from new journalists—Internet journalists who operate independently of traditional news gathering organizations. In some cases, bloggers act as reporters themselves—providing not only commentary but adding new and relevant information or insights to the debate over public issues. This may affect traditional journalists, perhaps spurring them to reemphasize aspects of reporting that have given way to covering celebrity trials and regurgitating official information. The more Internet journalists dig into government reports for clues on the effects of government policy, contrast conflicting official statements at different points in time, or file Freedom of Information Act requests for information that has been withheld, the more traditional journalists will need to do the same to avoid being embarrassed by these new competitors.

Internet journalism, however, continues to develop. Perhaps the same trends toward consolidation and bottom-line pressures that have sapped the aggressiveness of the mainstream media will eventually drain away the vigor of Internet journalists. Consolidation already has occurred with the creation of entities such as The Huffington Post, which has conglomerated smaller bloggers under one brand. The Internet has such low barriers to entry, however, that competition is likely to remain lively. Starting a new blog is much cheaper and easier than starting a new newspaper.

In the short run, blogs are having their largest impact on journalism through their press commentary. News criticism used to be the domain of a handful of professionals working for big city newspapers—the Howard Kurtzes of the world, for example. The advent of the blogosphere, however, opened up press criticism to news consumers in a way that has more possibilities than letters to the editor or op-ed pieces. Bloggers do not need the newspaper's permission to get their criticisms published. Nor do they need to wait until the next day's edition. Blogger criticism can ricochet around the net before a newscast has ended, as Dan Rather and CBS found out with their story on the National Guard memos regarding George W. Bush's service. Such blogging can mobilize news consumers to demand changes in coverage. When bloggers include the email addresses and telephone numbers of those responsible for news decisions, news organizations feel the heat like never before.

While conservative bloggers scored a hit on Rather and CBS, the progressive blogosphere has had its own successes. In December 2002, Josh Marshall revealed on his *Talking Points Memo* blog that in appearance at Strom Thurmond's 100th birthday party, then–Senate Majority Leader Trent Lott had seemed to endorse Thurmond's anti-segregation views of 1948. Marshall went on to chide the mainstream media for overlooking the story, bringing enough attention to the incident that Lott ultimately stepped down as majority leader.[62]

Since then, progressive blogs have continued to grow in reach, prompting Chris Bowers and Matthew Stoller to call them "a new force in American politics." In their study of the blogosphere, Bowers and Stoller report that although conservatives once dominated the online universe, progressive blogs have overtaken and surpassed them in traffic. As recently as July 2003, conservative blogs drew far more readers than did progressive ones. The most-visited blog was a conservative one, *Instapundit*, and conservative blogs overall had two to three times as much traffic as the progressive blogosphere. Within two years, the progressive blogosphere was generating nearly twice as much traffic as conservative blogs. By July 2005, the largest progressive blog, *Daily Kos*, had eclipsed *Instapundit* and was attracting quadruple the monthly visits of the former blogosphere king.[63]

Blogs now number in the millions, and their ranks continue to grow. A relative handful among them are widely read. Yet those that focus on media analysis and criticism are helping needle the mainstream media into both reclaiming their watchdog status and redefining their role in a digital society.[64]

The articles assembled here from progressive bloggers and Internet journalists cover only a few of the issues confronting American journalism and society. Yet they represent some of the most penetrating and well-thought-out critiques of the institution that is so fundamental to American democracy. Still, they offer only a starting point for thinking seriously about these issues. And think seriously about them we must because in many ways, the quality of our government is related to the vigor of our free press.

Notes

1. Edward R. Murrow, speech, Radio-Television News Directors Association and Foundation, October 15, 1958, Chicago, copy at The Association of Electronic Journalists web site (http://www.rtnda.org/resources/speeches/murrow.html).

2. "Edward (Egburt) Roscow Murrow," Old Time Radio - Radio Days web site (http://www.otr.com/murrow.shtml) accessed December 16, 2005); "Edward R. Murrow," American Masters Series, Public Broadcasting System web site, (http://www.pbs.org/wnet/americanmasters/database/murrow_e.html) accessed December 16, 2005.

3. Julie Morris, "The Man Who Fought McCarthy's Red Smear," *Detroit News*, "The Rearview Mirror," *Detroit News* web site (http://info.detnews.com/history/story/index.cfm?id-221&category=people) accessed December 16, 2005.

4. Ibid.

5. "Edward R. Murrow," American Masters Series, Public Broadcasting System web site (http://www.pbs.org/wnet/americanmasters/database/murrow_e.html) accessed on December 16, 2005.

6. Anna Everett, "The Civil Rights Movement and Television," in *Encyclopedia of Television*, Horace Newcomb, ed. (New York: Routledge, 2004) Museum of Broadcast Communications web site, (http://www.museum.tv/archives/etv/C/htmlC/civilrights/civilrights.htm) accessed on December 16, 2005.

7. Erika Tyner Allen, "The Kennedy-Nixon Presidential Debates, 1960," in *Encyclopedia of Television*, Museum of Broadcast Communications web site (http://www.museum.tv/archives/etv/K/htmlK/kennedy-nixon/kennedy-nixon.htm) accessed on December 16, 2005.

8. "The Pentagon Papers: Secrets, Lies, and Audiotapes (The Nixon Tapes and the Supreme Court Tape)" The National Security Archive, George Washington University web site (http://www.gwu.edu/~nsarchiv/NSAEBB/NSAEBB48/) accessed on December 17, 2005.

9. Doug Linder, "The Trial of John Peter Zenger: An Account," on Famous American Trials web site, University of Missouri at Kansas City

Law School (http://www.law.umkc.edu/faculty/projects/ftrials/zenger/zenger.html).

10. Daniel Ellsberg Bio, Ellsberg.Net –The Official Homepage of *Secrets: A Memoir of Vietnam and the Pentagon Papers* (http://www.ellsberg.net/bio.htm) accessed on December 17, 2005.

11. "Watergate" entry, "The American Presidency," Grolier Multimedia Encyclopedia web site (http://ap.grolier.com/article?assetid=0308470-0&templatename=/article/article.html) accessed on December 17, 2005.

12. Project for Excellence in Journalism, "Network TV—Audience" section of *State of the News Media 2005,* by Journalism.org, on State of the News Media web site (http://www.stateofthenewsmedia.org/2005/narrative_networktv_audience.asp?cat=3&media=4) accessed on December 18, 2005.

13. Deborah Starr Seibel, "News Svengalis at Work," May 30, 2005, Broadcasting and Cable web site (http://www.broadcastingcable.com/article/CA604567.html?display=Feature) accessed on December 18, 2005.

14. Neil Postman. *Amusing Ourselves to Death: Public Discourse in the Age of Show Business* (Penguin Books, 1985).

15. Project for Excellence in Journalism, "Network TV—Content Analysis" in *The State of the News Media 2005: An Annual Report on American Journalism,* on journalism.org web site (http://www.stateofthenewsmedia.org/2005/narrative_networktv_contentanalysis.asp?cat=2&media=4) accessed on February 9, 2006. The report suggests that election coverage drove down coverage of accidents, disasters, crime, business and the economy.

16. Arianna Huffington, "Just Say Noruba," June 20, 2005, The Huffington Post web site (http://www.huffingtonpost.com/theblog/archive/arianna-huffington/just-say-noruba_2928.html) accessed on February 9, 2006.

17. Project for Excellence in Journalism and Rick Edmonds, "Newspaper—Audience" section of *State of the News Media 2005,* by Journalism.org, on State of the News Media web site (http://www.stateofthenewsmedia.org/2005/narrative_newspapers_audience.asp?cat=3&media=2) accessed on December 17, 2005.

18. Jacques Steinberg, "Peter Jennings, Urbane News Anchor, Dies at 67," *New York Times*, August 8, 2005, http://www.nytimes.com/2005/08/08/

business/media/08jennings_obit.html?th&emc=th.

19. "Q & A: Weighing Anchor: As the Start of His Final Year, Tom Brokaw Takes Stock and Looks Ahead," January/February 2004, Columbia Journalism Review web site (http://www.cjr.org/issues/2004/1/QA-Brokaw.asp) accessed on February 9, 2006.

20. "Rather Candid About Bush National Guard Story," Marvin Kalb Interview of Dan Rather, The Kalb Report web site (http://www.gwu.edu/~kalb/) accessed on February 9, 2006.

21. "Talk Radio in America: Conservative vs. Progressive," Democracy Radio web page (http://www.democracyradio.org/survey) accessed August 22, 2005.

22. Bond quoted in Eric Alterman, *What Liberal Media: The Truth About Bias and the News* (New York: Basic books, 2003) 2.

23. Mark D. Watts, et al. "Elite Cues and Media Bias in Presidential Campaigns: Explaining Public Perceptions of a Liberal Press," in *Communications Research* 26:2 (April 1999) 144–175. Quotations from pp. 167–168.

24. Jane Hall, "Gore Media Coverage—Playing Hardball," in *Columbia Journalism Review* September/October 2000, on Columbia Journalism Review web page (http://www.cjr.org/archives.asp?url=/00/3/hall.asp) accessed on August 22, 2005.

25. "Our Current Howler (Part IV) Getting Gore Rewrite," March 2, 1999, The Daily Howler (http://www.dailyhowler.com/h032999_1.shtml) accessed on February 6, 2006.

26. "Fox Executive Spoke 5 Times with Cousin Bush on Election Night," The Associated Press, December 12, 2002, CNN web site (http://archives.cnn.com/2000/ALLPOLITICS/stories/12/12/tv.foxexecutive.ap) accessed on August 22, 2005.

27. Testimony of Roger Ailes, House Energy and Commerce Committee web site (http://energycommerce.house.gov/107/hearings/02142001Hearing216/Ailes320.htm) accessed on August 22, 2005.

28. Rob Garver, "Idiot Boxed," American Prospect Online Edition, October 4, 2004 (http://www.prospect.org/web/page.ww?section=root&name=ViewPrint&articleId=8540) accessed on August 22, 2005.

29. Jeff Cohen Interview, *Outfoxed: Rupert Murdoch's War on Journalism.* (Los Angeles: Robert Greenwald Productions, 2004).

30. "Rather's Retirement and 'Liberal Bias,'" March 2, 2005, Fairness and Accuracy in Reporting web site (http://www.fair.org/index.php?page=2460) accessed on August 23, 2005.

31. Steve Rendall and Tara Broughel, "Amplifying Officials, Squelching Dissent: FAIR Study Finds Democracy Poorly Served by War Coverage," May/June 2003, Fairness and Accuracy in Reporting web site (http://www.fair.org/index.php?page=1145&printer_friendly=1) accessed on August 23, 2005.

32. Crittenden quoted in Amy Goodman, *The Exception to the Rulers: Exposing Oily Politicians, War Profiteers, and the Media that Love Them* (New York: Hyperion Books, 2004) 175–176.

33. "The Times and Iraq," May 26, 2004, *New York Times* web site (http://www.nytimes.com/2004/05/26/international/middleeast/26FTE_NOTE.htm?ex=1124942400&en=a5f925335739b34e&ei=5070) accessed August 23, 2005.

34. Howard Kurtz, "Intra-Times Battle Over Iraqi Weapons," May 26, 2003, *Washington Post, Washington Post* web site (http://www.washingtonpost.com/ac2/wp-dyn/A39280-2003May25?language=printer) accessed on February 6, 2006.

35. Arianna Huffington, "Judy Miller: Do We Want to Know Everything Or Don't We?" July 27, 2005, Huffington Post blog web site (http://www.huffingtonpost.com/arianna-huffington/judy-miller-do-we-want-_b_4791.html) accessed on February 8, 2005. Huffington suggested that Miller may have been one of Libby's sources for Plame's identity as the wife of Joe Wilson, author of an op-ed piece in the *Times* debunking administration claims of an Iraqi effort to acquire nuclear weapons. Miller left the paper on November 9, 2005, after reaching a settlement with the newspaper prompted by the newspaper's decision to bar her from reporting. Katherine Q. Seelye, "Times Reporter Agrees to Leave the Paper," November 10, 2005, *The New York Times* web site (http://select.nytimes.com/search/restricted/article?res=F20715FE395A0C738DDDA80994DD404482) accessed on February 6, 2006.

36. Howard Kurtz, "The Post on WMDs: An Inside Story: Prewar Articles Questioning Threat Often Didn't Make Front Page," August 12, 2004, *Washington Post* web site (http://www.washingtonpost.com/ac2/wp-dyn/A58127-2004Aug11) accessed on February 6, 2006.

37. Kristin Borjesson, ed. *Feet to the Fire: The Media After 9/11: Top Journalists Speak Out* (Amherst, New York: Prometheus Books, 2005).

38. Page and Bumiller spoke at a November 4, 2004, panel discussion in Washington, D.C. sponsored by Northwestern's Medill School of Journalism. Quoted on Fairness and Accuracy in Reporting web site (http://www.fair.org/index.php?page=2481) accessed on August 23, 2005.

39. Jim Muir, "Journalists visit 'chemical weapons site,'" February 12, 2003, BBC News web site (http://news.bbc.co.uk/2/low/middle_east/2741003.stm) accessed on January 18, 2006.

40. The Associated Press, "Jayson Blair 'Couldn't Stop Laughing' Over Times' Correction," May 21, 2003, *Atlanta Journal-Constitution*, *Atlanta Journal-Constitution* web site (http://www.ajc.com/news/content/news/0503/21blair.html) accessed on December 19, 2005.

41. "CBS Ousts 4 for Bush Guard Story," January 10, 2005, CBS News, CBS News web site (http://www.cbsnews.com/stories/2005/01/10/national/main665727.shtml) accessed on December 19, 2005.

42. Howard Kurtz, "Newsweek Apologizes: Inaccurate Report on Koran Led to Riots," May 16, 2005, *Washington Post*, Washington Post web site (http://www.washingtonpost.com/wp-dyn/content/article/2005/05/15/AR2005051500605.html) accessed on December 19, 2005.

43. Howard Kurtz, "When Private Passions Meet Public Journalism," October 11, 2004, *Washington Post*, *Washington Post* web site (http://www.washingtonpost.com/wp-dyn/articles/A23086-2004Oct10.html) accessed on December 19, 2005.

44. Cliff Kincaid, "Cliff Notes," October 12, 2004, Accuracy in Media, Accuracy in Media web site (http://www.aim.org/aim_report_cliffs_notes/A2133_0_4_0/) accessed on December 19, 2005.

45. Project for Excellence in Journalism, "Overview-Ownership," *State of the News Media, 2004* , Journalism.org web site (http://www.stateofthemedia.com/2004/narrative_overview_ownership.asp?media=1) accessed on December 19, 2005.

46. Tom Fenton, *Bad News: The Decline of Reporting, the Business of News, and the Danger to Us All* (New York: Regan Books, 2005) 31–35.

47. Fenton, *Bad News*, 152–153.

48. Fenton, *Bad News*, 12.

49. Pew Research Center for the People and the Press, "Journalist Survey—Overview" from *State of the News Media 2004: An Annual Report on*

American Journalism, Journalism.org web site (http://www. stateofthemedia.com/journalist_survey_prc.asp) accessed on December 19, 2005.

50. Borjesson, ed., *Feet to the Fire: The Media After 9/11: Top Journalists Speak Out* (Amherst, New York: Prometheus Books, 2005), 44.

51. Eric Boehlert, "Katrina Jolts the Press: Why Has It Taken Thousands of Hurricane Fatalities to Finally Wake Up Reporters?" September 7, 2005, Salon.com (http://www.salon.com/opinion/feature/2005/09/07/press_katrina/) accessed on March 7, 2006; and Jay Rosen, "From Deference to Outrage: Katrina and the Press," September 9, 2005, PressThink blog (http://journalism.nyu.edu/pubzone/weblogs/pressthink/2005/09/08/ktr_aft.html) accessed on March 6, 2006.

52. Rosen, "From Deference to Outrage."

53. Kristina Borjesson, ed., *Feet to the Fire*, 167.

54. Borjesson, ed., *Feet to the Fire*, 33.

55. "2004 Facts About Newspapers," Newspaper Association of America web page (http://www.naa.org/info/facts04/circulation-daily.html).

56. Brian Stelter, "Jan. #'s: Total Viewers Vs. 2005," January 31, 2006, TV Newser, mediabistro web site (http://www.mediabistro.com/tvnewser/ratings/jan_s_total_viewers_vs_2005_31687.asp) accessed on February 9, 2006; Stelter, "Evening News Ratings: Week of Jan. 16," January 25, 2006, TV Newser, mediabistro web site (http://www.mediabistro.com/tvnewser/ratings/evening_news_ratings_week_of_jan_16_31367.asp) accessed on February 9, 2006. The cable ratings are averages for the month and the network ratings are averages for one week.

57. *State of the news media.*

58. Project for Excellence in Journalism, "Network TV" section of "State of the News Media: An Annual Report on American Journalism," journalism.org web site (http://www.stateofthenewsmedia.org/2005/narrative_networktv_intro.asp?media=4) accessed on February 9, 2006.

59. Project for Excellence in Journalism, "Newspapers—Economics," and "Newspapers—News Investment," from *State of the News Media 2005: An Annual Report on American Journalism,* journalism.org web site (http://www.stateofthenewsmedia.org/2005/narrative_newspapers_intro.asp?media=2) accessed on February 10, 2006.

60. "Andy Rooney: Schieffer 'Embarrassing' CBS News, January 12, 2006,

NewsMax web site (http://newsmax.com/archives/ic/2006/1/12/ 163755.shtml) accessed on February 8, 2006.

61. Dan Carroll, "Reassign NBC's Pete Williams," October 30, 2005, Huffington Post web site (http://www.huffingtonpost.com/dan-carol/ reassign-nbcs-pete-willi_b_9814.html) accessed on February 8, 2006; David Sirota, "Cheney Staffer-Turned-Reporter Now Covering Libby's Indictment for NBC News," October, 30, 2005, Sirotablog (http:// www.workingforchange.com/blog/index.cfm?mode=entry&entry= 42CA4708-D0AB-EDCC-7A5F370C730B573A) accessed on February 8, 2006.

62. Josh Marshall, Entries for December 6, 2002, and December 7, 2002, Talking Points Memo (http://www.talkingpointsmemo.com/archives/ week_2002_12_01.php) accessed on July 12, 2006.

63. Chris Bowers and Matthew Stoller, "Emergence of the Progressive Blogosphere: A New Force in American Politics," August 10, 2005, New Politics Institute web site (http://www.newpolitics.net/npi/blogreport .html) accessed on June 28, 2006.

64. Technocrati estimated the number at 14.2 million in August 2005, but the Technocrati site now says it is tracking well over 50 million sites. Dave Sifry, "State of the Blogosphere, August 2005, Part 1, Blog Growth," August 2, 2005, Technocrati website (http://www.newpolitics .net/npi/blogreport.html) accessed on September 13, 2006.

CHAPTER TWO

THE GREAT REWIRING:

internet media covers the media

WHERE THE MEDIA REVOLUTION (if you can call it that) leads is anyone's guess. This collection of readings tells the story from the point of view of the wired media—Internet journalists, activists, and bloggers.

Criticism of establishment media comes first, starting with Dan Rather's journalistic misdeeds, along with a little-noted story involving Carl Cameron's coverage of the 2004 election for Fox News. For Rather, problems were amplified by Internet media; in Cameron's case the story would not have existed were it not for the Internet. It's interesting to analyze how these two stories reflect on old media and new media. In Rather's case, his reporting on George W. Bush's National Guard service during Vietnam was a high-profile, old media (television) news story. When Rather's source for the story was seriously questioned, the story about the story blew up, culminating in Rather's resignation from CBS News. Cameron's false reporting, which really only ever played as a kind of parody, was written up on the Fox News web site and never broadcast or reported on an "old media" outlet. That Cameron (or someone at Fox News) was allowed to use the official web site in that way says something about the esteem old media outlets hold for Internet media. True, if Cameron's report had run on television, major media outlets would have aired commentary on it; as it was, it stayed more or less strictly on the Internet. For the time being, establishment media still holds the reins, but look at Joshua Marshall tell the story in detail as it unfolds and as he gets updates, hour by hour. There's a vitality in that kind of presentation—in turns insightful, then spontaneous, even glib—that other media have trouble pulling off.

These pieces are followed by critical commentary on coverage of the Iraq War and the "war on terror" in general. Media critics have repeatedly demonstrated instances of major media abandoning their watchdog role and allowing themselves to be the instrument of the government's version of the story (Eric Boehlert's *Lapdogs: How the Press Rolled Over for Bush* (Free Press) is one example of a book devoted to this topic). In this section, Jay Rosen uses coverage of The Downing Street Memo to consider the role of the Internet in keeping important stories alive until major media pay attention ("The Downing Street Memo and the Court of Appeal in News Judgment").

A third major theme of these posts addresses the myth of the liberal media. The "liberal media" story has been used to argue for the necessity of far right-wing talk shows and right-wing fundamentalist Christian radio (whose content could just as accurately be called political as religious)—the idea being that with all the liberal media (everything else), these formats provide "balance." Eric Alterman, author of *What Liberal Media?* has pointed out, however, that while reporters and journalists working in media are largely liberal, the owners and editorial boards are not. This editorial control over how news is presented helped to create a scenario where, for example, the *Washington Post* issued an apology for its reporting leading up to the Iraq War not by stating that the paper missed reporting that many intelligence officers questioned the real threat posed by Iraq, but rather by admitting that stories playing up the Iraq threat appeared as front-page news; more qualified analysis appeared on the inside pages, escaping notice of the casual reader, helping to create the illusion that the real story was the threat Iraq posed, not the honest questioning of the reality of that threat.

The concluding readings give some big-picture analysis of where media might go from here. Jeff Jarvis lays out ideas for major media to implement as they create presence on the Internet. By now, many of Jarvis' ideas are in fact being employed by big media; nearly every major outlet has a blog where reporters or editors interact directly with their readers, as one example. The final reading has Robert Parry addressing missteps made by progressive media in the past, showing that a better future is possible.

Along with all of the above, there are many other topics touched on. The variety of the featured readings shows the richness of the Internet as a news source. Here best-selling and award-winning authors commingle with relatively unknown newcomers whose readership is solely online. Some pieces are from conglomerate sites like *The Huffington Post* and *AlterNet;* some come from activist sites and independent blogs.

So yes, the conditions of the new media are unsettled, and where this leads is wide open for speculation. The articles here may make for some educated guesses.

A L T E R N E T . O R G

September 22, 2004

www.alternet.org

Rather Ridiculous

by John Nichols

JUST ABOUT THE ONLY sensible voice in the whole controversy over the documents CBS News used in its ham-handed attempt to raise questions about George W. Bush's "service" in the Texas National Guard came from retired typist Marian Carr Knox. As a former assistant to Lt. Colonel Jerry Killian, Bush's squadron commander who allegedly suggested that officers had been pressured to "sugar coat" their evaluations of the politically-connected young Guardsman, Knox was in a position to know more than just about anyone else about the authenticity of the documents and of the sentiments expressed in them. In interviews with several news outlets, including CBS, Knox suggested that the Killian memos were forged but accurate.

Now that CBS News anchor Dan Rather has acknowledged that he made a "mistake in judgment" when he relied on what now appear to have been bogus documents for a *60 Minutes* report that detailed some of the favorable treatment Bush received, Knox's seemingly strange statement offers one of the few realistic routes out of the thicket of spin the Bush administration has erected to avoid a serious discussion of the president's Vietnam-era "service" in the Guard.

Knox said she did not think the memos that were purported to have been written by Killian were genuine. But, she said, they reflected sentiments the National Guard commander expressed at the time. Thus, the documents that have caused such a stir as this year's presidential campaign enters its final weeks could indeed be both forged and accurate.

So where should Knox's insight lead us?

First, anyone who wants to know the truth about Bush's pampered "service" should be furious with Rather and the CBS crew. When they refused to follow basic fact-checking standards, they failed their viewers and the broader American public that would, for the first time, be exposed by the September 8 *60 Minutes* broadcast to a seemingly serious review of irregularities related to Bush's entry into the guard, his ignoring of direct orders, his failure to show up for duty and a pattern of reassignments that seemed always to benefit the son of a then-congressman from Texas rather than the country he was supposed to be serving.

After more than a month of virtually round-the-clock assessment of Democratic presidential candidate John Kerry's Vietnam service, major media has a responsibility to reexamine the president's controversial service record.

Yet, by doing a haphazard job of reporting and then rushing to broadcast the supposed "blockbuster" story, Rather and his crew played into the hands of a Bush spin machine that is now expert at peddling the lie that a liberal media is out to distort the president's record. While their intent may have been to shed light on an interesting and potentially significant story of the special treatment accorded this son of privilege, Rather and CBS, in their search for a "scoop," created a fog so thick that it could well obscure the story for the rest of the campaign.

By relying on a few documents that were not adequately verified, CBS handed White House political czar Karl Rove exactly what he needed to steer attention away from the real story. Of course it remains true that, as Rather says, "Those who have criticized aspects of our story have never criticized the heart of it . . . that George Bush received preferential treatment to get into the National Guard and, once there, failed to satisfy the requirements of his service."

Unfortunately, the "heart" of the story has been largely obscured by the controversy over the doctored documents.

As such, Rather and CBS are guilty of undermining not just their own story but the truth. That's particularly tragic because it was never really their story in the first place. The basic story of the machinations that George Herbert Walker Bush performed to help his son avoid serving in Vietnam, and the dirty details of the son's failure to do his duty as a Guardsman, was well reported almost five years ago by Texas columnist Molly Ivins and Texas investigative reporter Lou Dubose in their still-essential assessment of young Bush's path to power, *Shrub: The Short But Happy Political Life of George W. Bush* (Vintage). That book's chapter regarding Bush's Vietnam-era guard duty is exceptionally well-reported, compelling and, ultimately, more damning of the Bush family and the current president than anything produced since its publication.

So why didn't Rather and the CBS crew simply invite Ivins and Dubose, both experienced Texas reporters with long histories of sorting fact from fiction when dealing with the Bush family, to help produce a *60 Minutes* report that would have told the story accurately and thoroughly? Perhaps CBS executives thought that, because Ivins and Dubose write with a point of view, rather than feigning journalistic impartiality, they could not be trusted to get the straight story. That, of course, is the common bias of the elite broadcast media in the United States.

Unfortunately, that bias led Rather and CBS to produce a story that has done severe damage to the prospects that the great mass of Americans will ever learn the truth about their president's Vietnam-era actions. There is a lesson to be learned here: There was never any need for Rather and CBS to go searching for a "scoop" regarding Bush's time in the Guard. The story has already been reported and written by Ivins and Dubose. What there was a need for was a network with the courage to take that story, attach some pictures and broadcast it. Unfortunately, CBS proved incapable of performing that simple task. And, in so doing, CBS put the truth a little further out of reach for most Americans.

C O M M O N   D R E A M S
September 20, 2004
www.commondreams.org

The Lynching of Dan Rather: On British TV, Dan Feared the Price of "Asking Questions"
by Greg Palast

"IT'S THAT FEAR that keeps journalists from asking the toughest of the tough questions," the aging American journalist told the British television audience.

In June 2002, Dan Rather looked old, defeated, making a confession he dare not speak on American TV about the deadly censorship—and self-censorship—which had seized US newsrooms. After September 11, news on the U.S. tube was bound and gagged. Any reporter who stepped out of line, he said, would be professionally lynched as un-American.

"It's an obscene comparison," he said, "but there was a time in South Africa when people would put flaming tires around people's necks if they dissented. In some ways, the fear is that you will be necklaced here. You will have a flaming tire of lack of patriotism put around your neck." No U.S. reporter who values his neck or career will "bore in on the tough questions."

Dan said all these things to a British audience. However, back in the U.S.A., he smothered his conscience and told his TV audience: "George Bush is the President. He makes the decisions. He wants me to line up, just tell me where."

During the war in Vietnam, Dan's predecessor at CBS, Walter Cronkite, asked some pretty hard questions about Nixon's handling of the war in Vietnam. Today, our sons and daughters are dying in Bush wars. But, unlike Cronkite, Dan could not, would not, question George Bush, Top Gun Fighter Pilot, Our Maximum Beloved Leader in the war on terror.

On the British broadcast, without his network minders snooping, you could see Dan seething and deeply unhappy with himself for playing the game.

"What is going on," he said, "I'm sorry to say, is a belief that the public doesn't need to know—limiting access, limiting information to cover the backsides of those who are in charge of the war. It's extremely dangerous and cannot and should not be accepted, and I'm sorry to say that up to and including this moment of this interview, that overwhelmingly it has been accepted by the American people. And the current Administration revels in that, they relish and take refuge in that."

Dan's words had a poignant personal ring for me. He was speaking on *Newsnight*, BBC's nightly current affairs program, which broadcasts my own reports. I do not report for BBC, despite its stature, by choice. The truth is, if I want to put a hard, investigative report about the U.S.A. on the nightly news, I have to broadcast it in exile, from London. For Americans my broadcasts are stopped at an electronic Berlin wall.

Indeed, Dan is in hot water for a report my own investigative team put in Britain's Guardian papers and on BBC TV years ago. Way back in 1999, I wrote that former Texas Lt.

Governor Ben Barnes had put in the fix for little George Bush to get out of 'Nam and into the Air Guard.

What is hot news this month in the U.S.A. is a five-year-old story to the rest of the world. And you still wouldn't see it in the U.S.A. except that Dan Rather, with a *60 Minutes* producer, finally got fed up and ready to step out of line. And, as Dan predicted, he stuck out his neck and got it chopped off.

Is Rather's report accurate? Is George W. Bush a war hero or a privileged little Shirker-in-Chief? Today I saw a goofy two page spread in the *Washington Post* about a typewriter used to write a memo with no significance to the draft-dodge story. What I haven't read about in my own country's media is about two crucial documents supporting the BBC/CBS story. The first is Barnes' signed and sworn affidavit to a Texas Court, from 1999, in which he testifies to the Air Guard fix—which Texas Governor George W. Bush, given the opportunity, declined to challenge.

And there is a second document, from the files of U.S. Justice Department, again confirming the story of the fix to keep George's white bottom out of Vietnam. That document, shown last year in the BBC television documentary, "Bush Family Fortunes," correctly identifies Barnes as the bag man even before his 1999 confession.

At BBC, we also obtained a statement from the man who made the call to the Air Guard general on behalf of Bush at Barnes' request. Want to see the document? I've posted it at: www.gregpalast.com/ulf/documents/draftdodgeblanked.jpg.

This is not a story about Dan Rather. The white millionaire celebrity can defend himself without my help. This is really a story about fear, the fear that stops other reporters in the U.S. from following the evidence about this Administration to where it leads. American news guys and news gals, practicing their smiles, adjusting their hairspray levels, bleaching their teeth and performing all the other activities that are at the heart of U.S. TV journalism, will look to the treatment of Dan Rather and say, "Not me, babe." No questions will be asked, as Dan predicted, lest they risk necklacing and their careers as news actors burnt to death.

TALKING POINTS MEMO

October 1, 2004

http://talkingpointsmemo.com

---

by Josh Marshall

1:31 p.m. EDT—Is Fox News literally making stuff up out of whole cloth about John Kerry?

I DON'T EXPECT MUCH from this Republican operation. But this does seem to break new ground.

If you go to the front page of the Fox News site, there's a link right there up front to "Trail Tales: What's that Face."

Link through and you find this . . .

> Rallying supporters in Tampa Friday, Kerry played up his performance in Thursday night's debate, in which many observers agreed the Massachusetts senator outperformed the president.
>
> "Didn't my nails and cuticles look great? What a good debate!" Kerry said Friday.
>
> With the foreign-policy debate in the history books, Kerry hopes to keep the pressure on and the sense of traction going.
>
> Aides say he will step up attacks on the president in the next few days, and pivot some-

what to the domestic agenda, with a focus on women and abortion rights.

"It's about the Supreme Court. Women should like me! I do manicures," Kerry said.

Kerry still trails in actual horse-race polls, but aides say his performance was strong enough to rally his base and further appeal to voters ready for a change.

"I'm metrosexual—he's a cowboy," the Democratic candidate said of himself and his opponent.

A "metrosexual" is defined as an urbane male with a strong aesthetic sense who spends a great deal of time and money on his appearance and lifestyle.

Did Kerry really say that stuff? Stuff that sounds like classic winger parody? I looked around on Google and no other reporters seem to have gotten those choice quotes from Senator Kerry. A source on the Kerry campaign told me Kerry certainly didn't say anything remotely like that.

So what's the story from Fox? Are these quotes real? Made up? Unidentified parody? Straight-up fabrications?

1:54 p.m. EDT—Caught Red-Handed?

This morning on the Fox News web site, Fox was running a post-debate story about Kerry with several apparently fabricated quotes meant to disparage the Democratic candidate. (See the previous post for details.)

Some examples . . .

"Women should like me! I do manicures."

About himself and the president: "I'm metrosexual—he's a cowboy."

Now Fox has pulled the article from the front page without explanation. And on the article itself the passages I quoted in the [previous post] have all been removed—again, without explanation. [. . .]

So what's the deal here? Where did the fabricated piece come from? Who made up the quotes? How long did it run? Why did it get taken down? What happened?

2:40 p.m. EDT

Follow-up to the previous two posts . . .

I just placed a call to Fox News in Washington, D.C., to see if they had any explanation for the fabricated Kerry story they were running this morning on their web site.

We're waiting to hear back. We'll update when we hear their explanation.

Howie,[1] are you gonna be following up on this?

4:48 p.m. EDT

Okay, some more details on that bogus Kerry story that ran this morning on the Fox News web site. As we noted earlier, this morning the front page of the Fox web site ran a story with a series of phony Kerry quotes (see [previous post]). After questions were asked the offending material was quickly pulled from the site, without explanation.

So what happened?

Late this afternoon I spoke to Fox spokesman Paul Schur who told me the following . . .

"Carl [Cameron] made a stupid mistake which he regrets. And he has been reprimanded for his lapse in judgment. It was a poor attempt at humor."

So the Fox reporter covering the Kerry campaign puts together this Kerry-bashing parody right out of the RNC playbook with phony quotes intended to peg him as girlish fool and somehow it found its way on the Fox web site as a news item.

Imagine that.

More to follow . . .

5:08 p.m. EDT

Fox News has now posted a retraction and apology for the piece with the fabricated Kerry quotes . . .

> Earlier Friday, FOXNews.com posted an item purporting to contain quotations from Kerry. The item was based on a reporter's partial script that had been written in jest and should not have been posted or broadcast. We regret the error, which occurred because of fatigue and bad judgment, not malice.

The only retraction doesn't name the reporter in question, Carl Cameron, which was noted in the statement Fox News gave TPM this afternoon.

5:31 p.m. EDT

I will spare you any pretense of mock surprise that Fox News is ridiculously biased against the Kerry campaign. But it's one thing to know it and another to get such a blazing and undeniable example of it as a story with fabricated Kerry-bashing quotes put together by the Fox News reporter covering the Kerry campaign.

(Carl Cameron, the reporter in question, according to Fox spokesman Paul Schur, is Fox's "chief political correspondent.")

But it brings up a point raised in an article by Howie Kurtz a few days back.

On Monday Kurtz discussed a study by the Center for Media and Public Affairs that showed that Fox News coverage of Kerry was overwhelmingly negative.

Kurtz got these quotes from Cameron's boss Brit Hume . . .

Brit Hume, Fox's Washington managing editor, whose *Special Report* was examined by the study, says he's surprised by the anti-Kerry findings. "Our day-in, day-out coverage by Carl Cameron has been extremely fair to Kerry, and the Kerry campaign has recognized this," he says.

"We did a lot on the Swift Boat Veterans. We thought it was a totally legitimate story and found it an appalling lapse by many of our competitive news organizations that were treating that story like it was cancerous." But even there, Hume says, "we were abundantly fair to John Kerry's side."

"Extremely fair" to Kerry? "Abundantly fair" about the Swift Boat stuff?

The same reporter who made up these "Kerry quotes"?

- "Women should like me! I do manicures."
- "Didn't my nails and cuticles look great? What a good debate!"
- "I'm metrosexual—[Bush's] a cowboy."

Kurtz could do us all a favor and get Hume on the horn to see if he's still willing to call Cameron "extremely fair to Kerry."

October 2, 2004
11:18 a.m. EDT
Cuticle Carl?

12:29 p.m. EDT
A few questions and points about Carl Cameron's Kerry-bashing fabrications on Fox or A Guide for the Perplexed (media reporters) . . .

1. How long did the fabricated quotes run on the Fox News web site?
2. Fox News says Cameron has been "reprimanded."
   How? Are there any consequences? What happened to him? How was he reprimanded? Fox spokesman Paul Schur, who

first spoke to TPM yesterday afternoon, told *The Daily News* "We're simply moving on from this, we have no further comment." And that doesn't inspire a lot of confidence that the "reprimand" is anything more than a "Carl, don't post any more fabricated quotes on the web site." Meanwhile, Schur declined to tell the *LA Times* what if any discipline Cameron faced.

3. Just for the sake of discussion, can there be any question that Carl Cameron has contempt and disdain for John Kerry—contempt and disdain that he has great difficulty keeping a lid on?

4. Shouldn't Cameron be taken off the Kerry campaign beat? Assume for the moment that Cameron's fabricated story wasn't supposed to run on the site. If Cameron sits around writing up phony news stories only for Fox News colleagues which portray Kerry as a swishy fool, can he really credibly cover the campaign as a straight news reporter? The answer is obvious, I think. Of course, he can't.

5. Fox says Cameron made an "error" because of "fatigue and bad judgment." What was the error? Making up the fabricated quotes? Sending a Kerry-bashing parody around to colleagues at Fox News? Posting it on the web site as a news story?

6. Did Cameron post the material to the site himself, not realizing there was a problem? Or did a tech person or editor at the web site get a hold of Cameron's fabrications and post it not realizing it was a fabrication?

7. How tired is Carl Cameron and will Fox News be requiring him to get more sleep?

8. Why did comments very similar to Cameron's fabrications come up again and again from Fox commentators on debate night?

9. If CNN's John King posted a story on the CNN web site with fabricated quotes that had the president joking about funneling money to Halliburton or telling a crowd how only saps went to Vietnam, what would the fall-out or consequences be?

Notes for Talking Points Memo

1 "Howie" is Howard Kurtz, the well-known media analyst who writes the "Media Notes" column for *The Washington Post*.

M E D I A   M A T T E R S

October 4, 2004

http://mediamatters.org

Cameron's fake Kerry story capped Fox commentators' manicure fixation

by J.C.

AFTER FOX NEWS CHANNEL chief political correspondent Carl Cameron wrote a fake news story mocking Senator John Kerry that was published October 1 on FOXNews.com, blogger and journalist Joshua Micah Marshall posed a question to the network: "Why did comments very similar to Cameron's fabrications come up again and again from Fox commentators on debate night?"

As Marshall noted on October 1, the story as it originally appeared—part of a FOXNews.com "Trail Tales" report containing several other items—falsely attributed quotes to Kerry in an attempt to ridicule him over a manicure, which Cameron reported he received on September 30. Later that day, Fox News Channel issued a retraction and an apology, and the fake story was removed from the "Trail Tales" report. According to a *New*

York Times article, Fox News Channel spokesman Paul Schur said: "This was a stupid mistake and a lapse in judgment, and Carl [Cameron] regrets it."

Following are some of the fabricated quotations appearing in Cameron's fake story:

- "Didn't my nails and cuticles look great? What a good debate!" Kerry said Friday.
- "Women should like me! I do manicures," Kerry said.
- "I'm metrosexual—he's a cowboy," the Democratic candidate said of himself and his opponent.

But Cameron's fake news story was not the first sign of Fox's fixation on the purported manicure. Prior to the first presidential debate, Cameron reported on *Special Report with Brit Hume* that Kerry got "a pre-debate manicure." Fox News Channel hosts and contributors quickly picked up on Cameron's report, discussing the reported manicure five separate times in the three hours preceding the debate. No other cable news channel mentioned the topic.

From the September 30 edition of Fox News Channel's *Special Report with Brit Hume*:

> HUME: Carl, what's up with the manicure? Does he regularly get manicures?
>
> CAMERON: Not so regularly. But suffice it to say in his hotel spa, some of the ladies today were particularly amused and excited about their appointment with John Kerry to get him set up for tonight's debate.
>
> [. . .]
>
> HUME: I've had a manicure in my life. It was a rather pleasant experience. But do you think it was the thing to do today, perhaps?

SUSAN ESTRICH (Fox News Channel contributor and Democratic strategist): No! No! No! Look, I get my nails done all the time. I mean, I'm a fool for manicures. But obviously, what John Kerry needs to do tonight, among other things, is make a connection with average working people. And probably the way to start doing that is not with a manicure. Now, you've had them. But my guess is most men don't stop on their way to an important event with a manicure. But my hope is for John Kerry's sake, is that tonight people will forget about the manicure.

[. . .]

HUME: [W]e now know that he got a manicure today. According to Carl Cameron, he got himself a manicure today. What's up with that?

MICHAEL BARONE (Fox News Channel political contributor): I see nothing wrong with a manicure. I've been advised by friend to get a manicure. But I confess, I've never done so.

HUME: Well, I've had a manicure. It's not an unpleasant experience.

MORTON M. KONDRACKE (Fox News Channel co-host of *The Beltway Boys*): It's not what folks do out in the country is get a manicure. Why do they announce this kind of thing?

HUME: Believe me, they didn't announce it.

KONDRACKE: All right. Well, it's all right. Then it's silly that he would have done it.

FRED BARNES (*The Beltway Boys* co-host): This is a man who needs to stop windsurfing, stop getting a manicure and desperately needs to go bowling.

BARONE: Well, he does—I mean, this is a man who lives a lifestyle that's very dissimilar to that of the ordinary American person with five palatial houses.

HUME: You've got to wonder. This gesture, John Kerry, reporting for duty didn't work. I don't know that this will either.

From the September 30 edition of Fox News Channel's *The O'Reilly Factor*:

NEWT GINGRICH (Fox News Channel political contributor): Well, the first thing I would tell him [Kerry] to do is don't get a manicure. I can't imagine a dumber thing going into the debate than the last four hours of news broken, I think by Carl Cameron here on Fox News—because it makes him look silly. And it guarantees that everyone in the country's going to look at his fingers early in the debate. I know that sounds small, but it's the little thing like Dukakis in a tank that just doesn't come across right and sort of jars people who are looking for an excuse to vote for him.

O'REILLY: Well, he did the tan thing, too. He did the spray-on tan thing, which I thought wasn't very smart. I mean, my line was, gee, you know, what do you think Osama bin Laden's going to think about this spray-on tan? Is that going to frighten him? I don't know if it will.

[. . .]

PAT CADDELL (Fox News Channel contributor and pollster): I'll tell you what, as a

Democrat, I don't quite understand the fact
that, you know, while the president's out meeting with people who've been, you know, hurricane survivors, my candidate is out there
getting a manicure today and—

O'REILLY: No, the manicure thing—and the
tan thing, that was not good.

C O M M O N   D R E A M S

May 23, 2005

www.commondreams.org

Laundered, Spun and Hung Out to Dry:
The Real Lesson from Last Week's Riots

by John Atcheson

LAST WEEK, as the Muslim world boiled over with deadly rage,
the conservative spin machine, aided and abetted by an easily
exploitable press, once again captured the story, distorted the
message, and misled America. In their version of the truth, it's
all *Newsweek*'s fault.

Allowing the White House spin machine and the accompa-
nying chorus of right-wing echo chambers to portray the
Newsweek story as "the cause" of those lethal riots should have
ignited a firestorm of protest from the legitimate media. Indeed, the White House's posturing and the press's acceptance
of it is the most egregious abuse of journalistic ethics to come
out of the whole sad affair. And while a few in the media questioned whether it was accurate or fair to pin the blame on
Newsweek, their skepticism became a sideshow in what was essentially an orgy of censure by the right wing and ultimately
self-recrimination on the part of *Newsweek* and the press.

Just as with the Dan Rather affair, the balance of evidence suggests that *Newsweek's* story was accurate, even if the sourcing was sloppy. The mistreatment of the Koran had been widely reported previously by several newspapers, and verified by US interrogators, former prisoners, the International Red Cross, and others.

When conservatives succeed—again and again—in making the manner in which a story critical of their interests is reported the main issue, rather than whether the story is true or not, then careless sourcing is the least of our problems.

The plain fact is, the riots and the anger that sparked them was the inevitable result of the President's policies, not a single one paragraph story in *Newsweek*. And letting the White House and the conservative talk meisters get away with making *Newsweek* the fall guy for the consequences of this administration's policy failures is an offense against the journalistic canon far more serious than how news is sourced, and far more damaging to the media's credibility.

Let's look at the context, and the truths embedded within it. The Bush administration discarded the Geneva Convention and the rule of law in our dealings with Muslims. We've been guilty of torturing Arab prisoners; conducting illegal kidnappings under the rubric of "extraordinary rendition"; launching preemptive wars under false pretenses; assaulting the world with sanctimonious and arrogant lectures from the likes of General my-God-can-beat-up-your-God Boykin; and offering hypocritical support of corrupt Arab regimes in the face of high-blown rhetoric about championing freedom and democracy. We have abandoned Afghanistan to war lords and drug lords, and our failures in Iraq have allowed that country to descend into chaos, and in the minds of many Arabs, turned us into occupiers, not liberators.

Newsweek is just the latest victim in this administration's desperate attempt to find a scapegoat for their botched war on terror. The fact is, the so-called war on terror is ultimately a battle for the hearts and minds of the Islamic world, and Mr. Bush's strategy for waging that war is a policy fiasco of epic proportions.

As the Defense Policy Board said in a report released in September of 2004, outlining the failure of the US to win the war of ideas in the Muslim world, "Muslims do not hate our freedom, but rather they hate our policies."

DIA Director Lowell Jacoby outlines the depths of the administration's failure in testimony before Congress each year in his Global Threat Assessment. In 2004, he said, "Support for America has dropped in most of the Muslim world." Here's some of the chilling statistics he cited in that testimony, as well as some from a second poll conducted for the State Department in 2003. In Morocco, support for America dropped from 77% in 2000 to 27% by the Spring of 2003. In Jordan, it went from 25% in 2002 to 1% in May of 2003; in Saudi Arabia, it fell from 63% in May of 2000 to 11% in October of 2003. In Turkey, the number of people judging the U.S. favorably fell from 65% when Bush took office to 15% in 2003, and in Indonesia it fell from a high of 75% in 2000 to 15% by the end of 2003.

The White House has been willing to wag any dog, tell any tale, trump up any scapegoat in a desperate attempt to explain away or distract the country from the depths of its incompetence.

No doubt the press has been remiss in how it uses sources, particularly anonymous sources. But that failure pales in comparison to the much larger failure of the press allowing itself to be laundered, rinsed and hung out to dry by the Conservative spin machine. That's why the press's credibility is at an all-time low; that's why readership is down, and that is the most serious journalistic failure being illuminated by last week's riots.

Newsweek must account for its lapses, but if the press continues to allow itself to get spun by the White House and the right-wing whack jobs who routinely ignore truth, accuracy and context, then focusing on sloppy sourcing amounts to little more than wiping up a spilled glass of water, while a Tsunami is bearing down upon us.

B I G   E Y E

September 21, 2003

http://bigeye.com

Christine Amanpour Is Right About the U.S. Media

by Eric S. Margolis

MIAMI, FLORIDA—I'VE LONG CONSIDERED CNN's Christiane Amanpour an outstanding journalist.

Last week my opinion of her rose further when she ignited a storm of controversy when asked by a TV interviewer about US media's coverage of the Iraq War. Breaking a taboo of silence in mainstream media, Amanpour courageously replied, "I think the press was muzzled and I think the press self-muzzled. Television...was intimidated by the Administration and its foot soldiers at [a cable network]."

Right on cue, faithful to Reichsmarshall Hermann Goering's advice to slander all dissenting views as treason, the cable network accused Amanpour of being a "spokeswoman for al-Qaida." I felt for Ms Amanpour, having myself been slandered by the US neo-conservative media as "a friend of Saddam" for disputing White House claims about Iraq—whose secret police had threatened to hang me on my last visit to Baghdad.

The pro-war, neo-conservative *National Review*, whose flaccid mama's boys never seem to have served in their own nation's armed forces, actually had the nerve to call me, who volunteered for the US Army during the Vietnam War, "un-patriotic."

Christiane Amanpour is absolutely right, the US media was muzzled and censored itself. I experienced this firsthand on US TV, radio, and in print. Never in my twenty years in media have I seen such unconscionable pressure exerted on journalists to conform to the government's party line.

Criticism of the wars in Afghanistan and Iraq, photos of dead American soldiers or civilians killed by bombing, were forbidden. The tone of reporting had to be strongly positive, filled with uplifting stories about liberation of Afghanistan and Iraq, and women freed from Taliban repression. Criticism, sharp questions, and doubt about US policy were hushed up.

The bloated corporations dominating US media feared antagonizing the White House, which was pushing for the bill—just rejected by the Senate—to allow them to grow even larger. Reporters who failed to toe the line were barred from access to the military and government officials, ending their careers. "Embedded" reporters in Iraq and Afghanistan became little more than public relations auxiliaries.

Critics of Administration policies in Iraq and Afghanistan were systematically excluded from media commentary, particularly on national TV. Night after night, networks featured "experts" who droned on about Iraq's fearsome weapons of mass destruction that posed an imminent threat to the US, about Iraq's links to al-Qaida, the urgency to invade Iraq before it could strike at America, and a raft of other fabrications.

Such "experts" echoed the White House party line and all were dead wrong. Yet amazingly, many are still on air, continuing to misinform the public, using convoluted Talmudic arguments to explain why they were not really wrong even when they were wrong.

I do not exaggerate when I say that much of the US media from 9/11 to the present closely resembled the old Soviet media that I knew and disrespected during my stays in the USSR during the 1980s.

The American media, notably the sycophantic White House press corps and flag-wavers at cable TV news, treated President Bush and his entourage with the same sucrose adulation and fawning servility that Soviet state media lavished on Comrade Chairman Leonid Brezhnev.

When dimwitted Brezhnev made the calamitous blunder of invading Afghanistan, the Moscow media rapturously described the brazen aggression as "liberation" that recalled the glories of World War II. The US media indulged in the same frenzied foot-kissing, and the same silly WWII comparisons over Bush's foolhardy invasions of Afghanistan and Iraq. President Bush and his neo-conservative handlers led America into these twin disasters precisely because two of the key organs of democracy—an independent, inquiring media, and assertive legislature (Congress) failed miserably to perform their duty. They allowed themselves to be cowed into subservience. They failed to expose and vigorously oppose the sinister, proto-totalitarian Patriot Act that now so endangers America's basic liberties.

Or, like cable network TV, they eagerly served as White House mouthpieces, stoking war fever and national hysteria, retailing to the public all the Administration's wholesale disinformation about Iraq.

In a shocking attempt to silence dissenting voices, US forces bombed the news offices of the outspoken al-Jazeera TV in Baghdad, Basra, and Kabul, killing and wounding some of its staff. Independent reporters in Baghdad's Palestine Hotel were attacked and killed by US forces.

A leading Al-Jazeera correspondent, Tayseer Alouni, has been arrested in Spain and charged with aiding terrorism by interviewing Osama bin Laden. The US previously accused Alouni of being pro-Iraqi; Iraq expelled him for being "anti-Iraqi." In my book, that makes him an honest, courageous journalist, just like Ms Amanpour.

So long as Bush was riding high in the polls, the media fawned on him. The media always follows power. But now that many Americans are beginning to sense they were lied to or misled by the White House, Bush's popularity is dropping, and the media's mood is becoming edgy and more aggressive. Perhaps even vengeful. The muzzles may soon be coming off.

D A I L Y   H O W L E R

May 17, 2004

www.dailyhowler.com

Don't Look Back (Part 1)! Pundits snoozed on the road to Iraq. Jim Lehrer has a strange explanation

by Bob Somerby

WE WERE STRUCK by Jim Lehrer's remarks when he played a bit of *Hardball* last Wednesday. The PBS host has been making the rounds promoting his latest novel, *Flying Crows*—one of the novels he finds time to write in spite of his broadcasting duties. But talk of fiction would have to wait; Lehrer's host,

Chris Matthews, was talking Iraq. Early on, he asked a good question–after making an odd admission:

> MATTHEWS (5/12/04): During the course of the war, there was a lot of snap-to coverage. We're at war. We have to root for the country to some extent. You're not supposed to be too aggressively critical of a country at combat, especially when it's your own.
>
> And yet it seems something missing from this debate was a critical analysis of where it was taking us. That if you occupy a country for good or bad reason, you face resistance because of nationalism. It's always out there in every country, especially ours.
>
> You then face an underground. Then you have to fight an underground with the tactics that sometimes get ugly. You've got to interrogate, for instance. You've got to crack the underground. Do you think journalism, by the objective standards we have in this country, in the early part of the twenty-first century, should have included that kind of analysis?
>
> Did the press fail to provide that "critical analysis" in the months before Iraq?

Lehrer said the press *had* failed, then offered a novel explanation:

> LEHRER (*continuing directly*): I do. The word "occupation," keep in mind, Chris, was never mentioned in the run-up to the war. It was "liberation." This was a war of liberation, not a war of occupation. So as a consequence, those of us in journalism never even looked at the issue of occupation.
>
> MATTHEWS: Because?

> LEHRER: Because it just didn't occur to us. We weren't smart enough to do it. I agree. I think it was a dereliction of ours—in retrospective.

According to Lehrer, the nation's scribes "weren't smart enough" to foresee the problems of occupation. Soon, Lehrer expanded on his remarks. He gave an even more surprising explanation for the pre-war reporting:

> LEHRER: You touched on something else when you asked the question. Let's say a group of journalists had gotten onto that. It would have been difficult to have had debates about that going in, when the president and the government of the—it's not talking about "occupation." They're talking about—it would have been—it would have taken some—you'd have had to have gone against the grain.
>
> MATTHEWS: Right. You'd also have come off as kind of a pointy-head trying to figure out some obscure issue here.
>
> LEHRER: Exactly.
>
> MATTHEWS: Not good guys and bad guys.
>
> LEHRER: Negative. Negativism.

Could "courage" be the word Lehrer sought? Did he want to say: "It would have taken some *courage"* for the nation's press "to have gone against the grain" pre-Iraq? We were surprised to hear Lehrer say how "difficult" those debates would have been. Inevitably, we thought of Elisabeth Bumiller, explaining why Bush got softball questions in his last pre-war press conference (see *The Daily Howler*, 3/25/04):

> BUMILLER: I think we were very deferen-

tial because . . . it's very intense, it's frightening to stand up there. Think about it, you're
standing up on prime-time live TV asking the
president of the United States a question when
the country's about to go to war. There was a
very serious, somber tone that evening, and
no one wanted to get into an argument with
the president at this very serious time.[2]

According to Bumiller, it would have been "frightening" to
ask real questions. Now, Lehrer seemed to say it would have
been "difficult" to "go against the grain" at this time.

Let's give Lehrer credit for telling the truth, although his
remarks struck us as odd. But Matthews took his guest's comments in stride. Next, he asked about Lehrer's "brilliant
lifestyle"—and we thought the exchange might help you see
why the press corps is often so docile:

MATTHEWS (*continuing directly*): Let me
ask you about your brilliant lifestyle. I don't
know how you do it, Jim, because you are
very active socially. We bump into each other,
my wife and you, you guys, and I just have to
say, you write like a full-time novelist. And
you've done it again! Do you get up at 4 in
the morning and deny yourself a cup of cof-
fee for three hours until you've written 500
words or what? How do you do this? You've
done another great novel!

LEHRER: Chris, I am—I am blessed by having been in daily journalism for forty years.
This means writing is a natural act to me. I
think with my fingers. And I get up very—I
do get up, not quite at 4, but I do get up early.
And I go to my office a couple of hours before anybody else did. And I work every day.
The only way I can write these books—

> MATTHEWS: You're over there in Shirling-
> ton, Virginia.
>
> LEHRER: That's right.

Might we be permitted a question? If Lehrer had gotten up each morning and *studied the news* (see below), is there a chance he would have been "smart enough" to anticipate the problems of occupation? And if Lehrer cut back on that brilliant lifestyle—if he weren't so "active socially" among D.C. swells—might he have found it less "difficult" to conduct those debates we missed? Yes, Millionaire Pundit Values were in the air as Lehrer chatted with Matthews last week.

While Lehrer Slept: Let's state the obvious. It's absurd to say that "those of us in journalism never even looked at the issue of occupation" in the months before Iraq. Pundits may have chosen to ignore these concerns, but some reporters did report them. For example, here's part of a front-page report by Vernon Loeb and Thomas Ricks in the 3/11/03 *Washington Post*. (It took us about twenty seconds to find it.) Headline: "Iraq's Historic Factions May Severely Test a U.S. Occupying Force":

> LOEB AND RICKS (pgh 1): The U.S. Army is bracing both for war in Iraq and a postwar occupation that could tie up two to three Army divisions in an open-ended mission that would strain the all-volunteer force and put soldiers in the midst of warring ethnic and religious factions, Army officers and other senior defense officials say.
>
> (2) While the officers believe a decade of peacekeeping operations in Haiti, Somalia, the Balkans and now Afghanistan makes the Army uniquely qualified for the job, they fear that bringing democracy and stability to Iraq may be an impossible task.

The Doomsday Duo continued apace. "[T]he greatest source of concern among senior Army leaders is the uncertainty and complexity of the mission in postwar Iraq, which could require U.S. forces to protect Iraq's borders, referee clashes between ethnic and religious groups, ensure civilian security, provide humanitarian relief, secure possible chemical and biological weapons sites, and govern hundreds of towns and villages," they wrote. Maybe if Lehrer had put down his novels and picked up the *Post*, problems with post-war occupation might have "occurred to" the scribe.

A M E R I C A N   F R E E   P R E S S

April 6, 2004

www.americanfreepress.net

Media Coverage of Iraq Called "Shameful" by Peers

by Christopher Bollyn

IN THE ONGOING IRAQ CONFLICT, there is a growing realization among mainstream newsmen that they have failed the American public, but the U.S. military is happy with the way it controlled information through its program of embedding journalists with soldiers.

Those are just some of the outspoken assertions from a three-day *Media at War* conference at the University of California (Berkeley) School of Journalism. In attendance were Hans Blix, the former chief U.N. weapons inspector, Joseph Wilson, former U.S. ambassador to Iraq and a host of senior journalists and editors from the U.S. and abroad.

Serious criticism of the role of the U.S. media came from two leading journalists—Robert Scheer of *The Los Angeles Times*, who is a visiting professor at the journalism school, and John Burns, *The New York Times* bureau chief in Baghdad.

Scheer pulled no punches in making the following condemnation of his own profession: "This has been the most shameful era of American media. The media has been sucker-punched completely by this administration."

In making his contribution to the conference by phone from Baghdad, John Burns was equally forthright about where the blame should lie:

"We failed the American public by being insufficiently critical about elements of the administration's plan to go to war."

Maher Abdallah Ahmad of the Arab network, Al Jazeera, based in Qatar, said he felt that Americans still did not know what was happening in Iraq.

"Does anyone here know how many Iraqis were killed in the war? You make all these efforts to establish a democracy, and you don't give a damn how many people were killed?" he added.

The U.S. correspondent for Italy's *La Republica* newspaper Federico Rampini, told the conference he was amazed that American journalists have not investigated more deeply Vice President Dick Cheney's role in the Halliburton scandal. According to Rampini, such a story would have made the front pages for months in his native Italy.

"Frankly our job is to win the war. Part of that is information warfare. So we are going to attempt to dominate the information environment. Overall we were very happy with the outcome," Lt. Co. Richard Long told the conference. He was the former Marine Corps's public information director. In that role, he was responsible for the media "boot camp" at Quantico, Va., where 700 journalists were coached for the embedded process.

Responding to those comments, Todd Gitlin, professor of

sociology and journalism at Columbia University, pointed out that "embeddedness" has a tendency toward propaganda because a reporter is effectively part of the military team. The reporter's life therefore depends on the soldiers with whom he is embedded, and his desire to write negative stories is "quite diminished."

The debate about the U.S. media's failure to confront the Bush administration's case for going to war and the inadequacy of the overall coverage of the conflict have also found their way into ongoing exchanges in some parts of the media, including *American Free Press*.

In an article entitled "Now They Tell Us" in *The New York Review of Books*, Michael Massing vented his frustration in the following comments: "Where were you all before the war? Why didn't we learn more about these deceptions and concealments in the months when the administration was pressing its case for regime change; when, in short, it might have made a difference?"

Massing particularly focused on the *New York Times* writer Judith Miller, who wrote several front-page articles before the war about Iraq's alleged weapons of mass destruction (WMD), based on faulty information provided by Iraqi defectors of dubious credibility.

Massing pointed out that in an e-mail to John Burns, the *Times* bureau chief, Miller wrote that Ahmed Chalabi, the indicted bank embezzler and head of the exile Iraqi National Congress, "has provided most of the front page exclusives on WMD to our paper."

According to Massing, it was not until September 29, 2003, that *The New York Times* got around to informing readers about the controversy over Chalabi and the defectors associated with him.

"More than six months into the war and with no evidence

of the alleged Iraqi WMD anywhere to be found, Douglas Jehl reported that most of the information provided by Chalabi and his defectors had been judged by the Defense Intelligence Agency as being 'of little or no value.' The performance of the *Times* was especially deficient. Compared to other major papers, the *Times* placed more credence in defectors, expressed less confidence in inspectors, and paid less attention to dissenters," complained Massing.

When he personally asked Miller why she had not included more comments in her stories from experts who contested the assertions made by Iraqi defectors and the White House, she offered the following explanation:

"My job isn't to assess the government's information and be an independent intelligence analyst myself. My job is to tell readers of *The New York Times* what the government thought about Iraq's arsenal."

Miller's journalistic defense did not satisfy Rich Mercier of *the Free Lance Star* of Fredericksburg, VA. On March 28, he wrote the following:

"But even a cub reporter should know that if the government tells her the sky is blue, it's her job to check whether it might not be red or gray or black. And skepticism must be exercised most strongly when the matter at hand is whether the nation will go to war. By neglecting to fully employ their critical-thinking faculties, Miller and many of her colleagues in the elite print media not only failed their readers during the countdown to the Iraq invasion, they failed our democracy. And there's no excusing that failure."

In Massing's view, the *Times* set a pro-war tone on Iraq that many other papers followed. For him, that was the "pack mentality—one of the most entrenched and disturbing features of American journalism."

P R E S S T H I N K

June 19, 2005

http://journalism.nyu.edu/pubzone/weblogs/pressthink

The Downing Street Memo and the Court of Appeal in News Judgment

by Jay Rosen

NEWS JUDGMENT USED TO BE KING. If the press ruled against you, you just weren't news. But if you weren't news how would anyone know enough about you to contest the ruling? Today, the World Wide Web is the sovereign force, and journalists live and work according to *its* rules.

About the Downing Street Memo[1]—which I think deserves sustained news attention, real Congressional hearings, questions and answers at White House briefings, continued blogging, serious examination by all Americans (including the President's supporters) and the interest of future historians, essentially for the reasons articulated here[2]—I have one thought to contribute.

"News stories," Joshua Marshall [author of *Talking Points Memo* blog] once said, "have a 24-hour audition on the news stage, and if they don't catch fire in that 24 hours, there's no second chance." His observation appears in the Harvard Kennedy School case study on the fall of Trent Lott (published in March 2004).[3]

But that's not the way world works anymore. The 24-hour audition still happens, and the big winners are still big news. But now there is a Court of Appeal in the State of Supreme News Judgment, and everyone knows the initial verdict can be reversed. Reversal on appeal came last week for the Downing

Street Memo (now memos, plural[4]) about 45 days after the first story broke.

We should use the opportunity to understand how the court works. (Other cases include the fate of Trent Lott, and the Swift Boat Veterans for Truth.) For if the news judgment of journalists is not final anymore, this only reminds us that it was never good enough to *be* as final as once it was.

The traditional press is "no longer sovereign over territory it once easily controlled," I wrote in "Bloggers vs. Journalists is Over" (January 15 [2005]).[5] "Not sovereign doesn't mean you go away. It means your influence isn't singular anymore." The Court of Appeal for news judgment, which sits on the left sometimes, and other times on the right, is an example of that.

What journalists call news judgment used to be king. If the press ruled against you, you just weren't news. But if you weren't news how would anyone know enough about you (or care) to contest the ruling? That's what having singular influence was all about. The way it works today, the World Wide Web is the sovereign force, and journalists live and work according to *its* rules.

Now if there's something newsworthy coming out of the U.K. but neglected in America, the political blogs in America and other activists online keep talking about it. Quickly the story's unjust obscurity will reach a political player who can change that by acting in a newsworthy way, lending fresh facts and additional reason to cover the story.

By such means the appeal of news judgment starts to take shape. This happened within a week when [US Representative John] Conyers began circulating a letter to President Bush—signed by 88 Democrats—that demanded from Bush an explanation. The Knight-Ridder Washington bureau, increasingly a dissident voice on these matters, treated that letter as news in a May 6 report. (The signers were up to 122 by the time Conyers sent his letter.)

Players in politics, reading the blogs (or in the case of Conyers, writing for them[6]), pick up the chatter and amplify it. Radio talk show hosts, also reading the blogs, and getting the e-mails from activists, amplify the chatter some more. Columnists who weren't a part of the consensus pay attention, seeking vindication for their own judgment. And all these players together mount the appeal. They go into Supreme News Court and say: "the press denied us, but we have a case."

On June 7, for example, Jefferson Morley of *The Washington Post* (who wrote about the memo May 3 for *The Washington Post*, but only in the online edition) pointed out that "the so-called Downing Street Memo remains among the top 10 most viewed articles on *The Times* of London site." All those clicks are part of the appeals process. Web users are speaking. "Reader interest" (one factor in news judgment) is being shown. So too with calls and e-mails to ombudsmen at newspapers. These helped trigger Barney Calame's report about *The New York Times*'s coverage, and two Michael Getler columns about *The Washington Post*'s decisions.

At the *Star-Tribune* in Minneapolis, reader representative Kate Parry forwarded a reader's e-mail to Nation & World editor Dennis McGrath. She asked him if he knew anything about the story. Parry describes what happened:

> McGrath knew about the memo—but not from the traditional news wires. In this country, wire services had provided only a brief mention of it May 2 deep in a *New York Times* advancer on the British election. McGrath knew about it because he had started getting the e-mails, too.

He and his wire editors began watching for a wire story. A week later, they were still watching.

"We were frustrated the wires weren't providing stories on this," McGrath said. Finally, he gave up waiting for the wires and assigned reporter Sharon Schmickle to write about it—despite the geographic disadvantage of reporting from Minneapolis on a story breaking in London.

Parry added that the Downing Street Memo story had "played out almost identically to the Swift Boat Veterans for Truth story last year. McGrath learned about the group and its ads from the Internet long before the wire services offered stories. He had a local reporter do that story as well." That's the Court of Appeal in session.

In any successful appeal, when the press digs in and ignores the story, this creates a second story, the subject of which is faulty news judgment. It's usually phrased as a question: Did the (news) judges rule in error? (*Christian Science Monitor*, May 17: "Why has 'Downing Street Memo' story been a 'dud' in U.S.?") Howard Kurtz finally made the case Thursday. The question, *What about the Downing Street Memo?* had been asked so often, he wrote, it "forced the mainstream media to take a second look."

NPR's ombudsman Jeffrey Dvorkin told Salon, "It's a bigger story than we've given it. It deserves more attention." He added, "It may have been blog-induced in the beginning, but now it has legs of its own."

When the second look was taken, some key editors judged themselves at fault. *USA Today*'s senior assignment editor for foreign news, Jim Cox, said not reporting on the memo was a mistake. "I wish we'd had something in early on, and I wish we'd been able to move the memo story forward. I feel like we missed an opportunity, and that's my fault," he said to *Salon*'s

Eric Boehlert. Deborah Seward, AP's international editor, issued a statement, "There is no question AP dropped the ball in not picking up on the Downing Street Memo sooner."

That's called winning on appeal.

Mark Danner writes in the June 9 *New York Review of Books* that the ultimate importance of the leaked memo "has to do with a certain attitude about facts," namely that they can be "fixed around the policy," as the document states. He points out that this is "an argument about power, and its influence on truth."

Power, the argument runs, can shape truth: power, in the end, can determine reality, or at least the reality that most people accept—a critical point, for the administration has been singularly effective in its recognition that what is most politically important is not what readers of *The New York Times* believe but what most Americans are willing to believe.

I don't think the press has learned how to deal yet with "power shapes truth," or the extreme contempt for reason-giving the Bush Administration has shown on matters of war and peace. For example, in judging whether a story deserves further play the press will ask, "were the facts in it previously reported?" (a news test) rather than asking: Have the facts in it been successfully denied at the top? (which is a power-shapes-truth question.) Ultimately this confusion helps explain the original judgment that the memo was not news, *and* the success of the appeal.

Post-script, June 20: With "I don't get it" irritation, someone asked in comments: Why are you making such a big deal of the Downing Street Memos, which are "old" and second-hand news?

Here's one reply. A representative democracy requires an elected commander-in-chief not only to *have* reasons, but to *give* reasons, publicly, for what he chooses to do. This is all the more vital post-1945, where we Americans make war without officially declaring it in order to give the President a freer hand, suspending our own Constitution in the bargain.

With this war, the reason-giving part of the operation totally failed. But that isn't, as Jeff Jarvis says, "a scandal of bad PR."[7] No. If you think reason-giving is PR you have already lost the battle for public choice in politics. It is a basic failure of national legitimacy to have your reason-giving go so awry as it did with this war. If you are a Bush supporter, my view is you should be doubly concerned because, as things stand, actions in Iraq you believe fully legitimate have seen their official rationale (that is, their reason-giving) fail.

I don't agree with those who say that because no weapons were found, the war lacks all logic or legitimacy. It might have an alternative logic, a broader and more expansive rationale than: Saddam has weapons, he must be stopped. The broader case has been made, after the fact. Jarvis lists it, point-by-point, in his post. But that isn't what people voted for, or Congress "voted" on. Something went seriously awry in the reason-giving. (Dan Gillmor: "What Jeff fails to note is that Congress would never have backed the war so fecklessly had the phony WMD issue been off the table.")[8]

Just as some of you don't "believe" the big deal some of us are making about the Downing Street Memos, I don't believe your small deal making about the Memo's story of reason-giving and war. Doesn't ring true to me.

Notes for "The Downing Street Memo and the Court of Appeal in News Judgment"

1. The Downing Street Memo is reprinted in *The Sunday Times*, May 1, 2005: http://www.timesonline.co.uk/article/0,,2087-1593607,00.html.

2. Mark Danner, "The Secret Way to War," June 9, 2005, *The New York*

Review of Books: The Secret Way to War (http://www.nybooks.com/
articles/18034) accessed on May 29, 2006. In the piece, Danner
emphasizes the importance of the Downing Street Memo, saying "[. . .]
even as President Bush told Americans in October 2002 that he
'hope[d] the use of force will not become necessary'—that such a
decision depended on whether or not the Iraqis complied with his
demands to rid themselves of their weapons of mass destruction—the
President had in fact already definitively decided, at least three months
before [. . .]."

3. "'Big Media' Meets the 'Bloggers': Coverage of Trent Lott's Remarks at
Strom Thurmond's Birthday Party" is available online at http://
www.ksg.harvard.edu/presspol/Research_Publications/Case_Studies/
1731_0.pdf. The paper gives an account of how Trent Lott's racist
remarks at the event went largely unreported, but were picked up and
focused on by bloggers. Eventually, Trent Lott resigned as US Senate
Majority Leader as a result of that exposure.

4. John Daniszewski, "New Memos Detail Early Plans for Invading Iraq,"
June 15, 2005, *Los Angeles Times* web site (http://www.latimes.com/
news/nationworld/world/la-fg-britmemos15jun15,0,3650829.story)
accessed on May 29, 2006.

5. Jay Rosen, "Bloggers vs. Journalists is Over," January 15, 2005,
PressThink web site (http://journalism.nyu.edu/pubzone/weblogs/
pressthink/2005/01/15/berk_pprd.html) accessed on May 29, 2006.

6. John Conyers is an occasional contrubutor to the blog section of *The
Huffington Post* , http://www.huffingtonpost.com/john-conyers.

7. Jeff Jarvis, "Take a memo," June 20, 2005, BuzzMachine web site
(http://www.buzzmachine.com/archives/2005_06_20.html#009893)
accessed on May 29, 2006. Jeff Jarvis responds directly to Rosen:
"JEESH: I am amazed sometimes how literal one has to be in the
blogosphere. Yes, I said bad PR. It's a wry way to say he lied—yes,
indeed, he wanted to invade Iraq from the first and we all knew it—and
he would have been better off if he had told the truth. There, is that
clear enough?"

8. Dan Gillmor, "The Downing Street Memos, in Context," June 20,
2005, Bayosphere web site (http://bayosphere.com/blog/dangillmor/
062005/downing_street) accessed on May 29, 2006.

T H E   D A I L Y   H O W L E R

June 19, 2005

www.dailyhowler.com

Downing Street Bozo

by Bob Somerby

MAYBE NOW YOU'LL START TO BELIEVE the things we've said about Michael Kinsley and, by extension, about the fops who are running our mainstream press corps. In Sunday's *Post* (and *Los Angeles Times*),[1] Kinsley writes an astonishing column about the Downing Street Memo. Do a gang of millionaire fops drive our discourse? In case you didn't know that already, Kinsley sets out to prove it—in spades.

As noted, Kinsley discusses the famous Downing Street Memo; in it, a top adviser to Tony Blair seems to say that President Bush had decided on war with Iraq as early as July 2002 (and was "fixing" the facts and the intel accordingly). The memo appeared on May 1 in the *Times* of London; concerned citizens have been dissecting it from that day to this, even as the Washington press corps struggled to avoid all discussion. (Panel discussions about Kerry's grades at Yale were far more germane.) But good news! The great Kinsley has finally read the whole memo! Drink in the sheer condescension as he explains why he did:

> After about the 200th e-mail from a stranger demanding that I cease my personal coverup of something called the Downing Street Memo, I decided to read it. It's all over the blogosphere and Air America, the left-wing talk radio network: This is the smoking gun of the Iraq war. It is proof positive that Presi-

> dent Bush was determined to invade Iraq the
> year before he did so. The whole "weapons of
> mass destruction" concern was phony from
> the start, and the drama about inspections was
> just kabuki: going through the motions.

At the *Times*, Daniel Okrent always seemed to think it was beneath his dignity to receive e-mails from the herd, and Kinsley betrays the same condescension, grumping about the effort required to get him to do his job. Only after receiving demands from hundreds of "strangers" did he do what any citizen would; only then did he bother to read "something called the Downing Street Memo," the locution he uses to show his disdain for the people who asked him to function. And if you don't find yourself struck by Kinsley's bald condescension, we hope you'll find yourself insulted when you read his account of the memo's contents. "I don't buy the fuss," Kinsley writes. Then he starts to explain why that is:

> Although it is flattering to be thought per-
> sonally responsible for allowing a proven war
> criminal to remain in office, in the end I don't
> buy the fuss. Nevertheless, I am enjoying it,
> as an encouraging sign of the revival of the
> left. Developing a paranoid theory and pro-
> moting it to the very edge of national respect-
> ability takes a certain amount of ideological
> self-confidence. It takes a critical mass of citi-
> zens with extreme views and the time and
> energy to obsess about them. It takes a pro-
> motional infrastructure and the widely shared
> self-discipline to settle on a story line, dissemi-
> nate it and stick to it.

There you start to have it, readers! If you think the Downing Street Memo may show or suggest that Bush was determined to invade Iraq early on, you have "a paranoid theory" and "extreme views"—and "the time and energy to obsess about them." (This distinguishes you from Kinsley, who didn't have the time or energy to read the memo until forced.) Indeed, throughout his piece, Kinsley keeps saying that you're an "extremist" with "extreme views" if you're bothered by this memo's contents. Maybe now you'll believe what we've told you about this bizarre, fallen man.

Because omigod! Fairly quickly, Kinsley begins to explain what the memo said. Try to believe that Kinsley was once the brightest scribe in all Washington:

> [The memo is] a report on a meeting of British Prime Minister Tony Blair and some aides on July 23, 2002. The key passage summarizes "recent talks in Washington" by the head of British foreign intelligence (identified, John Le Carre-style, simply as "C"). C reported that "Military action was now seen as inevitable. Bush wanted to remove Saddam, through military action, justified by the conjunction of terrorism and WMD. But intelligence and facts were being fixed around the policy . . . There was little discussion in Washington of the aftermath after military action."
>
> C's focus on the dog that didn't bark—the lack of discussion about the aftermath of war—was smart and prescient. But even on its face, the memo is not proof that Bush had decided on war. It says that war is "now seen as inevitable" by "Washington." That is, people other than Bush had concluded, based on observation, that he was determined to go to war. There is no claim of even fourth-hand knowledge that he had actually declared this

> intention. Even if "Washington" meant ac-
> tual administration decision makers, rather
> than the usual freelance chatterboxes, C is
> saying only that these people believe that war
> is how events will play out.

We agree: This memo *doesn't* "prove" that Bush had already decided on war. By its nature, the memo is a limited document. It's a short summary of that Blair staff meeting, written by Blair aide Matthew Rycroft; in the part of the memo under discussion, Rycroft is summarizing what "C" (actually, Sir Richard Dearlove) said when he reported to Blair on his recent trip to Washington. Given all that, there's room for error when we interpret this memo. Rycroft could be misconstruing what Dearlove actually said in the meeting. And even if Rycroft captured Dearlove's meaning, Dearlove could simply be wrong in his assessment of what he heard in Washington. Meanwhile, Rycroft's memo is pithy, and therefore unclear. Did he really mean that Dearlove had said that Bush was faking ("fixing") the facts about Iraq? The memo can't explain its own meaning, and it can't serve as a transcript of the meetings Dearlove attended. But the D-Street memo plainly suggests that Bush had already decided on war, and it plainly suggests the possibility that the Bush Admin was jiggering facts to promote this decision. Kinsley is right—this pithy memo "is not *proof* that Bush had decided on war." But for reasons that are perfectly obvious, serious citizens have found it disturbing.

That said, how absurd is Kinsley's attempt to wish away this memo? In the *New York Times,* Douglas Jehl described the Washington meetings on which Dearlove was reporting to Blair. Dearlove "had met in Washington with senior American officials, including George J. Tenet, then the director of central intelligence," Jehl reported—and his account is not in dispute.

But Kinsley, engaging in world-class clowning, acts as if Dearlove was sent to DC to hang out at Starbucks and eavesdrop on locals. In the passage above, Kinsley wonders if Dearlove was simply discussing things he had heard from "the usual freelance chatterboxes." As he continues, Kinsley's clowning on this matter reaches the point of pure insult:

> Of course, if "intelligence and facts were being fixed around the policy," rather than vice versa, that is pretty good evidence of Bush's intentions, as well as a scandal in its own right. And we know now that this was true and a half. Fixing intelligence and facts to fit a desired policy is the Bush II governing style, especially concerning the war in Iraq. But C offered no specifics, or none that made it into the memo. Nor does the memo assert that actual decision makers had told him they were fixing the facts. Although the prose is not exactly crystalline, it seems to be saying only that "Washington" had reached that conclusion.

Readers, if you don't feel insulted by nonsense like that, you ought to stop reading altogether. Could a high school sophomore get away with such blather? In fact, Kinsley's claim here is simply inaccurate. In fact, the text of the memo *doesn't* say that "Washington" had reached the conclusions in question; the memo simply *doesn't say* who had reached these conclusions (text below). But again, Dearlove had been sent to Washington to meet with Tenet and other high officials. Unless Sir Richard has fried his brains, he wasn't reporting what he heard when he rode around Washington on the Metro, and he wasn't telling Blair what five-out-of-six House interns now thought. Yes—Sir Richard Dearlove had gone to DC to meet with "actual decision makers." It's absurd to think that the Downing Street Memo concerns someone else's great thoughts.

Nor is it likely that Dearlove was telling Blair what Americans *journalists* thought. But as he continues, Kinsley moves on to that absurd notion. Try to believe that he wrote this:

> . . . Although the prose is not exactly crystalline, it seems to be saying only that "Washington" had reached that conclusion.

And of course Washington had done so. You don't need a secret memo to know this. Just look at what was in the newspapers on July 23, 2002, and the day before. Left-wing *Los Angeles Times* columnist Robert Scheer casually referred to the coming war against Iraq as "much-planned-for." The *New York Times* reported Defense Secretary Donald Rumsfeld's response to an earlier story "which reported preliminary planning on ways the United States might attack Iraq to topple President Saddam Hussein." Rumsfeld effectively confirmed the report by announcing an investigation of the leak.

There! According to Kinsley, Dearlove was actually telling Blair what "[l]eft-wing columnist Robert Scheer" thought! And he was telling Blair about a report in the *New York Times*— information he only could get by spending a few days in Washington.

Kinsley's piece is insulting and mad, from its start right on to its finish. But then, this is the man who had never heard of PNAC (see THE DAILY HOWLER, 5/9/05), and this is the man who gets his economic information from "Meathead,"[2] at Hollywood parties (same link). Given Kinsley's serial cluelessness, are you really surprised that he had to be bullied by 200 strangers before he would even *read* this memo? That he offers open resentment against those who asked him to read it? That he calls them "extremists" for being disturbed by the memo, or that he offers this bizarro account of what Dearlove was saying to Blair? And do you start to see that we were right when we told you that Kinsley has crashed and burned—that he is now just another Millionaire Fop, just one more in the bizarre gang of hacks who run America's "press corps?"

Yep! To Michael Kinsley, you're an "extremist" with "a paranoid theory" and "time to obsess" if the Downing Street Memo disturbs you. And if you write and ask him to please do his job, you'll be met with his high condescension. But inevitably, this is the attitude that obtains when we empower a millionaire press corps—a national press whose opinion leaders are almost all multimillionaires. Indeed, when an e-mailer asked the *Post's* Robert Kaiser why the *Post* was avoiding this topic, he got this f*ck-you back-talk too.3 But so it will go if a millionaire class is allowed to run our national discussion. Marie Antoinette would have understood Kinsley. We hope that our readers do too.

TOUGH LITTLE RICH BOY CALLS NAMES: Note the way Kinsley name-calls throughout. Air America is a "left-wing talk radio network." Robert Scheer is a "left-wing columnist." Are you troubled by the memo? That makes you an "extremist" with "a paranoid theory." Here at THE HOWLER, we stay away from "right-wing" and "left-wing" ourselves, since the locutions provide more heat than light and imply an obvious criticism. Why do today's "TV liberals" argue so poorly? *Because these people aren't "liberals" at all!* Michael Kinsley is a millionaire fop. Reread his column, then tell us he isn't.

FOR THE RECORD: Here's the part of the memo which describes what Dearlove ("C") reported to Blair:

> C reported on his recent talks in Washington. There was a perceptible shift in attitude.

> Military action was now seen as inevitable.
> Bush wanted to remove Saddam, through
> military action, justified by the conjunction
> of terrorism and WMD. But the intelligence
> and facts were being fixed around the policy.
> The NSC had no patience with the UN route,
> and no enthusiasm for publishing material on
> the Iraqi regime's record. There was little dis-
> cussion in Washington of the aftermath after
> military action.

The passage starts, "C reported on his recent talks in Washington"—his talks with Tenet and other high officials. Do you
believe that Dearlove was telling Blair what "the usual
chatterboxes" were saying in Washington? According to the
memo, Dearlove reported that "[t]he NSC had no patience
with the UN route." According to Michael Kinsley, of course,
Dearlove may have picked this up while lounging at his hotel's
rooftop pool. How long will a free people put up with the
Kinsleys—with a tribe of poodles who deride them for caring
and insult them with garbage like this?

Notes for "Downing Street Bozo"

1. Michael Kinsley, "No Smoking Gun," June 12, 2005, *The Washington
   Post* web site (http://www.washingtonpost.com/wp-dyn/content/article/
   2005/06/10/AR2005061001705.html), accessed on May 29, 2006.

2. PNAC is The Project for a New American Century, a think tank
   comprised of many extremely influential policy makers (including Dick
   Cheney, Donald Rumsfeld, Paul Wolfowitz, and Douglas Feith) whose
   crowning acheivement to date has been to influence the US decision to
   overthrow and occupy Iraq. In Bob Somerby's post of May 9, 2005
   (http://www.dailyhowler.com/dh050905.shtml), he points out that as of
   October 24, 2004, Kinsley had no immediate recognition of what
   PNAC is. "Meathead" refers to Rob Reiner, the actor/director/political
   activist remembered by some for playing the role of a character called
   "Meathead" by Archie Bunker in the 1970s television series, *All in the
   Family*.

3. In an online discussion, an e-mailer asked *Washington Post* journalist Rober Kaiser why his paper avoided the Downing Street Memo, asking "What's up with that?" Kaiser replied, "Robert G. Kaiser: What's up with you? Can you read? Did you read Walter Pincus's excellent journalism on that memo?" Online here: http://www.washingtonpost. com/wp-dyn/content/discussion/2005/06/06/DI2005060600529.html

---

P O P   M A T T E R S

July 16, 2003

www.popmatters.com

No Question the Media Is Right
by David Sirota

IT USED TO BE BIG NEWS when leaders were dishonest. The media forced politicians of both parties to pay a price for even the slightest infraction. Just ask Al Gore, who was tarred and feathered for a few careless comments about the Internet. That has changed. The media now barely flinches when the truth is distorted. In just a few years, the same media that tenaciously attacked the last White House over the tiniest appearance of impropriety now barely reports when the current White House deceives, hides information and knowingly ignores hard facts.

Take the White House's explanation of the deficit. On April 24th, President Bush said, "This nation has got a deficit because we have been through a war." Then, a week later, he said, "We've got a deficit because we went through a recession." The White House and the media know both of these explanations are dishonest—Bush's own budget acknowledges that his tax cuts are the major cause of the deficits (in table S-3 of Bush's budget, the White House acknowledges that without Bush's tax cuts the nation would return to surplus by 2006, but with his tax cuts deficits will continue indefinitely). Nonetheless, despite the doubletalk, the media did not report the story that the President was being dishonest.

Or how about the White House's assertion that "92 million Americans would receive an average tax cut of $1,083" under its economic plan? Again, the facts are seriously distorted in order to fool the public. In reality, 80 percent of taxpayers would receive less than $1,083, and half would receive $100 or less. The handful of millionaires who would get about $90,000 artificially inflates the average. The White House and the media know this, yet the misinformation continues unreported.

Why are these and countless other distortions swallowed by the media and fed to the American public without question?

CROOKED TIMBER

"Doesn't Ring a Bell" by Ted Barlow
www.crookedtimber.org
December 9, 2003

EVERYONE *KNOWS* THAT NBC's *Today* Show is liberally biased. Which is why it's interesting that in their segment on the manslaughter conviction of Rep. Bill Janklow, they didn't use the word "Republican."

Uggabugga has the audio file.* I don't think that I've ever watched the *Today* show, and I certainly wouldn't try to use this as evidence of conservative bias. I used to have frequent arguments about the impossibility of "proving" media bias by cherry-picking examples from the hundreds of hours and thousands of pages of media produced every day. But given the intellectual integrity of the most prominent right-leaning media watchdogs, all I can say is: Live by the anecdote, die by the anecdote.

* The blog *uggabugga* linked to the source audio file: http://members.dslextreme.com/users/markpoyser/uggabugga/2003/Janklow-on-NBC.wav.

First, in a post-9/11 world, the White House has effectively equated questioning of the Bush Administration with treason. White House spokesman Ari Fleischer threatened reporters after the attack, saying they "should watch what they say." More recently, Fleischer implied that reporters were being disloyal to the military by questioning why the President felt it necessary to hold a circus stunt photo-op on the deck of an aircraft carrier. "It does a disservice to the men and women of our military to suggest that the president, or the manner in which the president visited the military would be anything other than the exact appropriate thing to do," he said, just after admitting that he had been dishonest in saying the President actually needed to fly a jet to the ship.

But these tactics only go so far. What truly allows the White House distortions to go unreported—or reported as fact—is the Republican Party's not-so-secret weapon: a 24-hour television, radio and newspaper advertisement, otherwise known as Fox News, Clear Channel radio and the *Washington Times*. These national "news organizations" are owned by Australian billionaire Rupert Murdoch, longtime GOP benefactors Tom and R. Steven Hicks, and Reverend Sun Myung Moon of the Unification Church, respectively. These men are right-wing ideologues who take their radical agenda as seriously as their bottom lines. Their news staffs reflect this disposition (Just look at Fox News, whose CEO and news director is Roger Ailes, who before entering journalism was a major Republican Party political operative, and who informally advised Bush on post-September 11th image polishing). These ideologues understand that, devoid of effective ideas, conservatives can win by playing dirty—namely, by infiltrating non-partisan journalism with attack machines that use the pretense of objectivity as a cloak for pressing a radical right-wing agenda and diverting critical reporting away from the Bush Administration. As one Fox executive admitted a few months ago in *Fortune* magazine: "[Murdoch] hungered for the kind of influence in the United States that he had in England and Australia. Part of our political strategy here was [sic] the creation of Fox News."

Thus, legitimate questions about the war become a news hook for Fox to attack questioners as traitors. Inquiries about whether the President is adequately protecting the homeland become a chance to question Democrats' patriotism. Suggestions that the Bush tax cut will expand the deficit are morphed into purported schemes to raise taxes. Republican tax cuts for the wealthy become altruistic efforts to "let people keep more of the money they earn," as one Fox correspondent reported. Senate Democratic Leader Tom Daschle is hammered by the media for daring to question America's diplomacy, while Newt Gingrich gets favorable coverage when he does the same. In short, the right-wing media promote stories that serve conservative interests and deflect attention from stories that do not. In the process, they make incessant yet baseless claims that other news outlets are "liberal," intimidating them into accepting this conservative viewpoint for fear of being further vilified. And in "pack mentality" news with fierce ratings competition, the result is a media establishment that now forsakes its watchdog role in a tectonic ideological shift to the right.

As the next election nears, honest reporters and editors do a disservice to the public by accepting this manipulation. Americans deserve Woodward and Bernstein journalism—not O'Reilly and Hannity propaganda. We need our media to have the guts to tell us when, why, and how our government is misleading us on the nation's most pressing issues. Otherwise, our democracy suffers as Americans go to the polls without the knowledge required to cast an informed vote.

THE HUFFINGTON POST

November 1, 2005

www.huffingtonpost.com

Chris Matthews and the Hardball Gang

by Sheldon Drobny

AFTER THE SENATE DEMOCRATS today finally had the courage to play hardball with the Republican majority,[1] I turned on the TV to watch what the pundits would say about this. I first watched Wolf (the U-boat commander) Blitzer on CNN. Wolf guided his audience into a display of the typical for and against viewpoints of both Democrats and Republicans.

As I expected, there was no substance in this report nor was there any discussion about the need in general for the Senate Intelligence Committee to conduct the second phase of its report. The first phase was unanimously adopted, which reported to the Senate that there were a series of intelligence failures regarding the information that led us to war. To use a metaphor from the movie *Casablanca*, the Senate in its phase I report was "shocked that the intelligence was so bad." Phase II of the report was supposed to tell us if the Bush Administration had any responsibility for misleading the Congress and the American people by manipulating false intelligence about WMDs. That report was delayed for almost two years before the Democrats finally had some courage today.

I then turned to *Hardball* with Chris Matthews. *Hardball*'s panel included Andrea Mitchell, Nora O'Donnell, and Howard Fineman. I almost threw up while I was watching this group agree that this was a "tactic" used by the Democrats to keep the pressure on the White House and not allow Bush to change the subject with diversions such as the nomination of Judge

Alito and the Avian Flu vaccine. Not once did any of these pundits ever discuss that the American people are entitled to further discussion and investigation about the lies that led us to the war in Iraq. Not once did they say that the Republicans are obviously disingenuous about delaying this report and that the delay has been dictated to them by the White House. No, these professionals led by Matthews chastised the Democrats for not doing their job three years ago when many of them voted for the war resolution.

We all agree that many Democrats did not do their job three years ago. Many of us wonder why Senators Kerry, Clinton, Biden and others will not say that if they knew then what they know now, they would not have voted for the war. Perhaps they are waiting for this report to be completed before they make such a statement. So Matthews and his team played "hardball" with the Democrats for using this so-called "tactic." And that is the problem with the Corporate media. They always want to go backwards and they treat politics as if it were a game. I was taught to recognize mistakes and move forward. If the Senate Democrats are doing something positive today, what is the relevance of bringing up a past mistake? For the Corporate media, the relevance is to stir up the pot and create a false debate as if this were World Federation Wrestling. There should be no debate. The Senate Democrats are doing the right thing after the Libby indictments. Americans have every right to an explanation for such an obvious deception that has cost the lives of over 2000 Americans, many thousands more Iraqis and at a financial cost of hundreds of billions of dollars. I do like Howard Feinman a lot and I understand that he has to play it safe when he is on NBC and MSNBC. But, in this case, the issues of war and peace should out-trump those personal pressures.

The only really honest viewpoint came from Jack Cafferty of CNN, hardly one who is perceived as a liberal. He had the courage to say that this act by the Senate Democrats was a matter of "what is right or wrong" and not about any political "tactic" or political "game." I wonder whether Matthews will ever understand this.

Notes for "Chris Matthews and the Hardball Gang"

1. On November 1, 2005, Senate Minority Leader Harry Reid forced the Senate into closed session with a rarely used parliamentary move, threatening to shut down Senate business indefinitely unless Republicans who run the chamber agreed to follow through with an investigation by the Senate Intelligence Committee on the failures in intelligence prior to the war in Iraq.

TOMPAINE

November 21, 2005

www.tompaine.com

Woodward's Weakness

by Russ Baker (www.russbaker.com)

[Ed. Note: After Special Prosecutor Patrick Fitzgerald indicted Scooter Libby in the CIA leak case, Bob Woodward announced he had testified that a senior administration official told him about CIA operative Valerie Plame and her position at the agency nearly a month before her identity was disclosed.]

WHATEVER BOB WOODWARD DID or didn't do, should or shouldn't have done, knew or didn't know, several lessons can be drawn from this latest of media scandals—and none of them speak well of journalism as it is practiced at elite levels today.

For one thing, the very definition of an "investigative reporter," as Woodward is labeled these days *ad nauseum*, is a pretty elastic one. Meeting a source in a parking garage as a way of identifying abuses and high crimes by powerful insiders is one thing. Dining off that for the next three decades while chumming it up with well-placed insiders for their "exclusive accounts" is another.

In my book (and in most journalism textbooks), investigative reporting—as distinguished from other journalism—involves self-propelled inquiry into secrets that need to be uncovered. True investigative reporters struggle to obtain confidential or hard-to-obtain documents; elicit whistleblower testimony from those who could get in trouble for talking; track down elusive and obscure sources of valuable information; and undertake painstaking, time-consuming efforts to construct elaborate charts and timelines based on hundreds or thousands of disparate elements. It is exhausting, often unglamorous work, not usually carried out within easy reach of champagne or $100 meals.

Investigative journalism rarely involves asking powerful people what they think or how they would like to characterize their actions. And that's really what Bob Woodward has been doing for a long time: he has the fame and manner to gain access to sovereign and court jester alike, he gets them talking, and then he sells books full of what they have to say. Whether they are telling the truth, we have no way of knowing, because analysis and perspective are not Woodward's strong suits. And reporters who produce a book a year can't be doing a whole lot of investigating.

Woodward's investigative appetites are further called into doubt by his claim to have realized his first-place finish in the Valerie Plame leak sweepstakes only after he watched Patrick Fitzgerald's indictment press conference. If he were as savvy and interested as he suggests, he would have been preparing timelines based on the case since last summer at least, and therefore would have long recognized he could and would be a central player in the scandal.

Equally improbably, he asserts that by the time he thought fit to tell his boss (in late October) that he too had spoken in 2003 with White House officials about Plame, he was belatedly but "quite aggressively reporting" a story related to the Plame case. But why did it take the Libby indictment to prod him into aggressive-reporting mode when he himself had been privy to White House leaks whose only purpose was to discredit critics of the administration's false WMD claims? In media appearances, he'd long pooh-poohed Fitzgerald's investigation, while dismissing the outing of Plame altogether as a "non-story."

Notwithstanding his newly declared enthusiasm for the story, one has to wonder what might be the outcome of the "aggressive reporting" he is now engaged in. Something that incriminates high White House officials? Not likely, or there will be no more insider access—not with this administration, in any case. Besides, that "aggressive reporting," based on his track record, probably means more conversations with the players themselves—conversations that are more likely to comprise artful positioning on the part of the players rather than true confessionals.

There's a self-serving aspect to so much of this business. "I explained in detail that I was trying to protect my sources," Woodward said in an interview this week. "That's job number one in a case like this." What went unsaid was that protecting his sources—while maybe in the public interest—is definitely in his, since his entire genre is based on serving the interests of the powerful enough that they will continue to give him the unusual access that has made him rich.

The still-aborning Woodward controversy (with all the words already spoken and published in just a few short days) tells us something else about today's breed of superstar journalists (and the wannabes): Given a choice between uncovering elusive but crucial new insights, or merely commenting on the work of others, they will often choose the latter. Not that reporters are proscribed from taking shots—this article certainly qualifies—but the basis for the criticism ought to be a track record of seeking the truth about the WMD disinformation campaign itself—and not merely playing telephone within the make-believe world of the DC snowglobe.

The same can be said about coverage of Patrick Fitzgerald. I suspect that the journalist-hours so far devoted to speculation about Fitzgerald and what his grand juries might be up to far outweigh the time and effort spent investigating the underlying story: exactly how the Bush administration got us—America and the world—into the mess we're in.

Finally, there's Woodward's universally acknowledged special status. He is an "assistant managing editor" who does no managing, no editing and precious little daily journalism at all, but gets to carry a business card from a major daily while churning out bestseller insider tell-all books and earning a fortune for public speaking. The reality is that *The Washington Post* is a for-profit business, and so is Bob Woodward. Together, based mostly on advance excerpts from his books, they make money. Whether the public benefits—really truly benefits—as it does from fearless, exhaustive, plain vanilla investigative journalism is another question. (Other Posties do the real heavy lifting, but you've never heard of those poor schlubs.)

On Sunday, in a piece that was relatively tough on the wayward son, the *Post's* own ombudsman referred to Woodward as "a relentlessly aggressive reporter and a rock-solid member of the Washington Establishment"—a characterization that gives a whole new meaning to the term oxymoron. Woodward's knack for making nice with the people he should be unafraid to offend is evidence anew that journalism must be reformed, rather dramatically, if it is to survive. Let the reformation begin . . . right now.

CRANKY MEDIA GUY
July 7, 1999
www.crankymediaguy.com

The Irrelevancy of the Constitution
by The Cranky Media Guy

As THE OLD JOKE GOES, I love humanity, it's people I can't stand. Actually, with me, it's the other way around. I like people singly or in small groups, but humanity as a group? Scary and getting scarier all the time, Boss.

My favorite bumper sticker/T-shirt slogan of all time? "Never underestimate the power of stupid people in large groups." Truer words have never been spoken. Whereas I merely suspected the truth of this before, I now have absolute, undeniable confirmation of it. Would you like me to share, Brother?

This past Sunday, I was reading a story in my local paper (*The Free Lance-Star* of Fredericksburg, Virginia, just in case you're wondering) about the public's attitude toward the press. It was an AP story about some egghead group called the First Amendment Center at Vanderbilt University that asked people what they thought about freedom of the press.

The first part said that 53 percent think that the press has too much freedom. Think about that for a minute. A *majority* of American adults think that the press has "too much free-dom." Um, ex-*cuse* me? Later in the story, I read that only 65 percent think that newspapers should be able to publish freely without government approval of a story. That's when I *really* lost it.

In case you ever wondered, yes, I actually *do* believe the stuff I say in these columns. I really *am* cranky in person. When I read that last little statistic, I was ranting and raving and scar-ing the rest of the Cranky Family. Down deep, I really, *really* want to believe that humanity is worth saving, but I keep stub-bing my metaphorical toe on depressing stuff like this article.

If you're wondering why this was so upsetting to me, may I humbly suggest that you stop reading right now and go turn on the TV. Right about now, QVC is selling some magnetic shoe inserts that, although as the crawl says "are not yet recog-nized as effective by the medical community," are still sup-posed to relieve your back ache. (One afternoon, I watched in fascination as the QVC lady shill reassured me and all her view-ers that these insoles had the "bipolar magnets" in them. I don't know about you, but I, for one, absolutely *refuse* to buy any magnets that aren't bipolar. If you don't understand what's stu-pid about this, I sentence you to a month of watching *Bill Nye, The Science Guy*.)

If you're still here and haven't reached for the phone to buy those nifty shoe inserts yet, I'm assuming that you, also, are distressed by American citizens so fucking stupid that they ac-tually WANT the government—the same government run by the same politicians that they tell pollsters they distrust—to censor the news. At least I hope you are.

For the moment, let's put aside the absolute stupidity of someone who claims to be a freedom-loving American want-ing the government to prescreen their news for them. I mean, how Forrest Gump–like do you have to be to not see that we just recently wrapped up a nearly half-century "Cold War" against a political system that, among other things, censored the news its citizens could read? Remember that that was one of the Big Things we said was *wrong* about Communism? If it was wrong for *them*, what would make it right for *us* to do? (Okay, so I *didn't* "put it aside." I'm a little worked up here.)

Since conservatism seems to be the "default setting" of American politics (if you ask an American, even one who knows absolutely nothing about politics, what his persuasion is, chances are he'll say "conservative"), I'm gonna assume that many of the people who answered this poll consider themselves to be conservatives. Isn't one of the Big Principles of conservatism that the government should be as small and unobtrusive as possible? In that case, I have a question. "Hey, Mr. So-Called Conservative Who Wants to Censor the News Media," I'd ask (in that charming way that I have). "Exactly how big a bureaucracy do you think it would take to pre-read and approve or censor every news story in advance and who's gonna pay for this?"

I figure, since the news is a 24-hour-a-day thing nowadays, you'd have to have three big shifts of civil servants seven days a week checking every story coming across the wire. The tab for that's gonna add up pretty quick, don't you figure? Why, it would be almost like the old Soviet Union (Remember them? They were the "Evil Empire" Reagan said was Bad with a Capital B 'cause it did nasty stuff like restrict people's access to information), where it's estimated that one out of every three people worked for the government.

Even if you're *so* stupid that you still think government censorship of the news is a good idea, I'm assuming you wouldn't want to pick up the tab for this in the form of a higher tax bill.

Well, guess what, Sparky? If you *really, really* want that, you can have it since we are, at least in theory, still a democracy, but it ain't gonna be cheap. Totalitarianism never is. You gotta pay the Secret Police real well if you want to keep their loyalty. With the potential tab running to multi-billions a year, you *still* want a Ministry of Information? If you answered "Yes" to that question, you are hereby barred from ever again calling yourself a "conservative." From now on, the correct term to use is "fascist."

Wanna know what the real problem is? It isn't that the press has too much freedom. That's nonsense. It isn't that the press reports too much on what's wrong with the government. If anything, it's the opposite of that. With the huge mega-mergers in the communication industry, what you're seeing, for my money, is way too much *cooperation* on the part of the press and government. If you want to make sure that the Justice Department doesn't look too closely at your merger, what better way than to assure the Powers that Be that you won't make too much noise about any scandals that might rear their ugly little heads? The closer we get to monopolies in mass communication, the more the power to report is also the power to suppress information. It's the ol' Quid Pro Quo, boys and girls. One hand washes the other. You scratch my back, I'll scratch yours. Call it what you want.

Wait a minute. Know what? I'm a jerk. I'm sitting here typing this tirade and I *could* be putting together a business venture that would make me a fortune. If 53 percent of American adults want a censored newspaper, why not just *give* it to them? I mean, that's a hell of a big demographic, isn't it? I doubt I'd have trouble finding some branch of the Federal government to censor what went into my paper, if I promised them I'd only run what they approved. Shoot, I'll bet if I asked real nice, they'd *give* me the stories in the first place. That would save me the trouble and expense of having reporters.

This is brilliant! Why am I wasting my time on this "Cranky Media Guy" hobby BS when I could be the next Rupert Murdoch? If you can't fight 'em, join 'em, right? Okay, that settles it, I'm gonna do it! Be watching for my new, government-approved paper, coming soon to a newsstand near you. I've even come up with a catchy name for it: Pravda.

PUNDIT PAP

October 16, 2001

www.americanpolitics.com/punditpap.html

Kicking a Corpse—
The Whore Media might do what Osama bin Laden could not: Destroy American freedom

by Bryan Zepp Jamieson

Oct. 16, 2001—MT. SHASTA, CA (APJP)—ANYONE FAMILIAR with my essays knows that for some time, I have considered the mainstream American media—CNN, Faux, the television networks, and so on—to be corporate disgraces to journalism, interested not in dispensing information but only in ratings, and hopelessly corrupted by their corporate overlords.

Indeed, in my news service, the large majority of the news items I run are from foreign sources: England's *Guardian*, for instance, or the *Toronto Globe and Mail*, or even *Pravda*. There are few Americans over the age of forty who would have ever guessed that *Pravda* might tell us more about what is happening in America than the *New York Times*—but here we are.

If there was ever much doubt that I was justified in my

disdain for America's once-proud media, there were two stories over the past few days that should convince anyone not only that the corporations have sold Americans out entirely, but that America no longer has a free and independent press—or rather, it does, but it's small, and largely drowned out by noisy whores working for Murdoch, Isaacson, Moon, and Scaife, and owned by corporations such as Disney, GE, and Time/Warner/AOL—the same corporate class that, by and large, owns the government, too.[1]

In the first instance, Condoleezza Rice, Putsch's administration harpy, summoned the press and bade them to not show Osama bin Laden on television. The given reason almost made sense. He might be passing instructions along in code. Anyone who has read Kurt Vonnegut's novel, *Mother Night*, or seen the superb Nick Nolte movie of the same name, is familiar with the concept. Prearranged hesitations, coughs, chuckles, and choice of words can be used to pass along information outside the text stream.

But when bin Laden broadcasts, it's via satellite—which means that all the terrorists in America need is a satellite dish, a tuner box, and the Arabic version of TV Guide, and they can catch all bin Laden, all the time, in color, stereo, and close-captioned. Which means that the people who Condoleezza Rice putatively wants to prevent from getting the information aren't affected at all—while the American public find that the corporate media, and the illegitimate junta in Washington, are conspiring to control further what Americans get to see and hear.

NBC's head news whore, Neal Shapiro, made the amazing statement:

> . . . was that here was a charismatic speaker
> who could arouse anti-American sentiment

getting 20 minutes of air time to spew hatred
and urge his followers to kill Americans.

I dunno, Neal.

To tell you the truth, I think bin Laden's followers in America already hate Americans and want to kill them. It's not the kind of thing where you need to remind them: "Oh, and by the way, Mohammed, stop by the Quik-E-Mart and pick up a dozen eggs and some beer, and be sure to release some vials of cyanide in the subway at noon tomorrow."

As for the rest of us, I doubt bin Laden is going to make much in the way of inroads. I watched his broadcast from what Maureen Dowd called "the set of the Flintstones movie" for about ten minutes with a totally unprotected brain, and not once did I feel any urges to hijack a commercial jetliner and fly it into any prominent buildings. Not once.

In fact, bin Laden reminded me of nothing so much as some skinny old weirdo who comes up to you at a stoplight with a filthy, greasy rag in hand, and wants to know if he can clean your windshield for a dollar. If you let him make eye contact, he'll start ranting about the Zionist conspiracy, and how the CIA has put eavesdropping devices in his turban. Charismatic he's not—and I suspect most Arabs figure him for a dip, too, but since he's not the one bombing Afghanistan, they have to more or less support the crazy son of a bitch.

Rupert Murdoch, who has done more than any single individual in the history of the earth to destroy freedom of the press, made the incredible statement: "We'll do whatever is our patriotic duty."

Keep in mind: this was spoken by an Australian son of a bitch with a whore citizenship who openly bribed the Speaker of the House in order to get several billion dollars worth of stations in America in his grasp, and spent the past eight years doing everything he could to destroy the President of the United States.

"Patriotic duty?" Take your "patriotic duty" and ram it up your sleazy ass, Murdoch. We don't need to hear from scumbags like you about "patriotic duty."

CNN chief Walter Isaacson added, "After hearing Dr. Rice, we're not going to step on the landmines she was talking about." He probably sidled up to her afterward and apologized for his reporters having asked questions.

And the ever-thuggish Ari Fleischer demanded that papers not print the full text of Osama's speeches, since it might contain code.

Say—maybe they should just shut newspapers down entirely!

If Arab terrorists can use code, anyone can. For all Ari knows, this message is actually addressed to a vast armada of space ships lying in wait on the far side of the moon, awaiting only my command before wreaking endless death and destruction. ("Pl, hvzt. Pqfo gjkf. Gjwf cvdlt jg zpv ijv Bsj gjstu.")

The old saying has it that "The first casualty of war is truth," and thus this particular story wouldn't be too horrific. At various times in history, the media have gotten swept up in the wave of war fever patriotism, and deliberately muzzled itself in the cockeyed notion that America will benefit from it. Usually, they quickly realize that the government finds that far too convenient a relationship not to abuse, and the bloom is off the rose. In this case, they'll eventually figure out that we don't even really have a war!

But the second item is catastrophic for America, and signals that we have already lost America as we knew it.

The *Toronto Globe and Mail* broke the story on October 10, 2001. It begins as follows:

> U.S. media forget about dimpled chads
>
> By John Ibbitson
>
> Thursday, October 11, 2001 - Print Edition, Page A1
>
> WASHINGTON—Just weeks ago, it would have been the biggest story in the land: A final, comprehensive audit would reveal whether Al Gore or George W. Bush should be president. Today, it seems to be nobody's news.
>
> A consortium of major U.S. news organizations has decided unanimously not to analyze and report the results of the $1-million (U.S.) audit they commissioned to identify which presidential candidate received the most votes in Florida in last November's election.
>
> By "spiking" the story, they have raised questions about whether the country's biggest media conglomerates are suppressing news that potentially could tarnish the image of Mr. Bush in the midst of the President's war on terrorism.
>
> "I find it truly extraordinary that they have made this decision," said Jane Kirtley, media ethics specialist at the University of Minnesota. "I am so chilled by what is going on."
>
> Catherine Mathis, vice-president of corporate communications at the New York Times Co., reportedly said, "Right now, we don't have the time, the personnel or the space in the newspaper to focus on this." The consortium consists of *The New York Times, The Washington*

Post, The Wall Street Journal, Associated Press, *Newsweek,* CNN and several other news organizations.

No time, personnel, or space in the papers. Right. They could cover blowjobs 24/7 for a year and a half, but they don't have space to cover a coup against the United States.

Steven Goldstein, vice-president of corporate communications for Dow Jones & Co., which publishes *The Wall Street Urinal,* said, "The priorities have changed. People are focused on the fact that we're at war."

We're bombing the set of the Flintstones for no apparent reason—that's the "war" Goldstein is talking about, and it didn't stop the rich white trash on the WSJ editorial staff from pressing hard for such pet projects as cutting capital gains taxes or privatizing social security to be added to the anti-terrorism bill.

But what it boils down to is the fact that the whore media—*The New York Times*, *The Washington Post*, *The Wall Street Journal,* The Associated Press, *Newsweek*, CNN and several other news organizations—have unilaterally decided not to print the results of a completed survey because it would just upset people.

That can only mean one thing: George W. Putsch, indeed, lost Florida, and probably by a substantial margin.

If he had won, nobody would have been upset. I would have grumbled that he tried to steal it anyway, but I'll be the first to admit that it would be a grumble that would convince very few people. Republicans are sleazebags who cheat (shrug). Are you SURPRISED or something?

So the result must show that Gore won.[2]

Of course, the whore media are "trying to protect". . . well, somebody. They say America. I say they are trying to protect their milk cow, the Putsch junta. They say America is in crisis, and so they shouldn't print upsetting news. Wouldn't be right. Certainly wouldn't be "American."

In 1972, we were fighting in Vietnam. Did that stop the press from reporting on Watergate? During the civil war, Union newspapers carried livid accounts of the incompetence of our drunken and cowardly generals. Nobody questioned their patriotism for doing so. During World War I, many American papers blasted Wilson on a daily basis for getting America involved in a European war. Nobody condemned them for upsetting the country—not even Wilson.

The difference? In those wars, we didn't have a carnival media owned outright by cowardly and corrupt corporations who are intent on protecting their puppet regime in Washington at all costs.

It looks, more and more, like America lost, and well before the first plane smashed into the World Trade Center. It may be that Osama bin Ladin did nothing more than kick a corpse.

Notes for "Kicking a Corpse—The Whore Media might do what Osama bin Laden could not: Destroy American freedom"

1. Jamieson is referring to Rupert Murdoch, owner of Fox News Channel; Walter Isaacson, head of CNN; the Reverend Sun Myung Moon of the Unification Church, which owns the *Washington Times*, and Richard Melon Scaife, a Republican billionaire who has made sizable grants to right-wing publications such as the *American Spectator*. The Walt Disney Company owns ABC Television, General Electric Co. owns NBC, and Time/Warner/AOL owns CNN.

2. In fact, Gore won Florida, and hence the 2000 election, according to analysis by eight news organizations, as Robert Parry discusses in the following post, "Big Media, Some Nerve!" and in his *Consortiumnews. com* post "Gore's Victory," online at http://www.consortiumnews.com/ 2001/111201a.html. In the words of David Podvin and Carolyn Kay: "The eight news organizations were *The New York Times*, *The Washington Post*, Dow Jones and Company (*The Wall Street Journal*), the Associated Press, The Tribune Company (*The Los Angeles Times* and *The Chicago Tribune*, among others), *The Palm Beach Post*, *The St. Petersburg*

Times, and CNN (which later dropped out)." Online at http://www.
makethemaccountable.com/coverup/Part_02.htm.

CONSORTIUMNEWS.COM

November 13, 2004

www.consortiumnews.com

Big Media, Some Nerve!

by Robert Parry

YOU MIGHT THINK that the major media that got suckered by George W. Bush's Iraqi weapons-of-mass-destruction claims just last year would show some humility about its own fallibility.

But, no, the elite U.S. news media is now criticizing common citizens who have raised questions about voter fraud in the Nov. 2 election. *The New York Times* has joined the *Washington Post* and other major news outlets in scouring the Internet to find and discredit Americans who have expressed suspicions that Bush's victory might not have been entirely legitimate. *The New York Times'* front-page story was entitled, "Vote Fraud Theories, Spread By Blogs, Are Quickly Buried." [November 12, 2004.]

As odd as these attacks might seem to some, this pattern of protecting the Bush family has a history. It actually dates back a couple of decades, as the major media has either averted its eyes or rallied to the Bushes' defense when the family has faced suspicions of lying or corruption. [This pattern is detailed in my new book, *Secrecy & Privilege: Rise of the Bush Dynasty from Watergate to Iraq.*[1]]

That was the case in the 1980s when then–Vice President George H.W. Bush was implicated in a string of scandals, starting with the clandestine supplying of Nicaraguan contra rebels.

When one of Oliver North's secret supply planes was shot down over Nicaragua in October 1986, the surviving crew member, Eugene Hasenfus, correctly named Vice President Bush's office and the CIA as participants in the illegal operations. But for years, the big media accepted Bush's denials and dismissed Hasenfus's claims.

After the Nicaraguan contras were implicated in cocaine trafficking—when Vice President Bush was in charge of drug interdiction—again *The New York Times* and other leading publications pooh-poohed the stories. They even put down then-freshman Senator John Kerry when he investigated. However, the charges again turned out to be true, as CIA inspector general Frederick Hitz concluded in a little-noticed report a decade later. [For details, see *Consortiumnews.com*'s "Kerry's Contra-Cocaine Chapter."[2]]

Arming Saddam

When George H.W. Bush was linked to the misguided strategy of covertly arming Iraq's Saddam Hussein in the 1980s, again major U.S. news outlets—with the exception of the *Los Angeles Times*—did little to dig out the truth. Even today, after the junior George Bush has sent more than 1,100 U.S. troops to their deaths to clear Iraq of non-existent WMD stockpiles in 2003–04, the U.S. news media won't tell the American people about the senior George Bush's role in helping Hussein build a real WMD arsenal in the 1980s.

During the eight-year Clinton-Gore administration, shoddy reporting from *The New York Times* and the *Washington Post*—about President Clinton's Whitewater "scandal" and about Al Gore's supposed exaggerations in Campaign 2000—helped pave the way for the Bush Family's restoration. [See *Consortiumnews. com*'s "Al Gore vs. the Media" or "Protecting Bush-Cheney."[3]]

The big news organizations couldn't even get the stories straight about their own Florida recount in 2001. After examining all legally cast votes in Florida and finding that Al Gore should have won that crucial state—regardless of what chad standard was used—*The New York Times* and other news outlets buried the lead that Gore—not Bush—deserved to be president.[4]

Since these unofficial recount results were released in November 2001—after the September 11 attacks—the news organizations apparently thought it was best not to clue in the American people to the fact that the sitting president had really lost the election. So the news organizations spun their stories to Bush's advantage by focusing on a hypothetical partial recount that excluded so-called "overvotes," where voters both checked a box and wrote in the candidate's name, legal votes under Florida law.

After reading those slanted "Bush Won" stories, I wrote an article for *Consortiumnews.com* noting that the obvious lead should have been that Gore won. I suggested that the news judgments of senior editors may have been influenced by a desire to appear patriotic at a time of national crisis. [See *Consortiumnews.com*'s "Gore's Victory."[5]]

The article had been on the Internet for only an hour or two when I received an angry phone call from *New York Times* media writer Felicity Barringer, who accused me of impugning the journalistic integrity of then-*Times* executive editor Howell Raines. I was surprised that the mighty *New York Times* would be so sensitive about an Internet article that had questioned its judgment.

Professional Pressures

Having worked in mainstream Washington journalism for much of the last quarter century, however, I certainly understood—and even sympathized—with the pressures that reporters and editors face.

Especially when challenging Republicans and conservatives, journalists can expect to be accused of lacking patriotism, undermining national unity or having a "liberal bias." Beyond those ideological assaults, there's also the formidable pressure that the Bush family's gold-plated connections can bring down on a journalist's head.

Yet, while it may be understandable for national journalists to go easy on the Bushes, that pattern over the years has eroded public confidence in the media's fairness and integrity. Millions of Americans now flatly don't trust the national news media to tell the truth when the Bushes are involved.

That perception, in turn, has led rank-and-file Americans to step forward via web sites to lend whatever knowledge and expertise they have to investigate this powerful family. As amateurs, these Americans are sure to make mistakes or jump to conclusions that aren't well supported by facts.

But the big media has no moral foundation upon which to criticize these shortcomings by common citizens. If the professional journalists focused more on doing their jobs, rather than protecting their careers, the American people would be far better served.

notes for "Big Media, Some Nerve!"

1. Robert W. Parry, *Secrecy and Privilege: Rise of the Bush Dynasty from Watergate to Iraq* (Arlington, Va.: The Media Consortium, Inc., 2004).

2. Robert Parry, "Kerry's Contra-Cocaine Chapter," October 29, 2004, *Consortiumnews.com* web site (http://www.consortiumnews.com/2004/102904.html) accessed on May 29, 2006.

3. Robert Parry, "Al Gore vs. the Media," (http://www.consortiumnews.
   com/2000/020100a.html) and "Protecting Bush-Cheney" (http://
   www.consortiumnews.com/2000/101500a.html), both from the
   Consortiumnews.com web site.

4. Robert Parry, "Gore's Victory," November 12, 2001, *Consortiumnews
   .com* web site (http://www.consortiumnews.com/2000/101500a.html)
   accessed on May 29, 2006.

5. Ibid.

R E P U B L I C A N P R E S S

June 12, 2005

www.republicanpress.com

Slanted Liberal Media Poll: Bush Approval is Down

by RepublicanPress.com Staff

A RECENT POLL by the liberal Associated Press and the ultra-liberal Ipsos [the global market research firm] showed President Bush's overall approval rating dipping to 43%. But, the Fox News/RepublicanPress.com poll done by The 700 Club shows that more Americans think President Bush is doing a good job.

"The liberal media is out to get President Bush by creating a poll that shows their outrage at President Bush," said a senior 700 Club pollster who wished to be identified as Chubby Checker to preserve his anonymity. "One just has to look at how the questions were worded to see that it was a poll skewed to the left," Chubby Checker went on to say.

The staff at RepublicanPress.com looked at the poll sponsored by the liberal Associated Press and the ultra-liberal Ipsos. We found that the questions asked were liberally slanted, and in some cases were found to have some type of brainwashing effect on the participant. The questions caused the participating person to become unpatriotic, disheartened, and dismayed at basic Republican morals and values.

"We are at war and these silly polls are giving aide and comfort to our enemies!" was the response from the White House.

Our own poll conducted by the 700 Club showed 98% thought President Bush was doing a good job, while only 2% thought he wasn't. The poll went on to show that 97% of real Americans were Bush supporters. Only 2% of those polled by 700 Club thought President Bush was a piece of human excrement. Those who dislike President Bush were 10 times more likely to consider themselves either flag burners, fags, commies, or pro-abortion. These same respondents were up to 5 times more likely to go see a Jane Fonda movie.

"Polls go up and polls go down," said a professor at Jerry Falwell's Liberty University. "Our own poll shows more Americans are pleased with President Bush and his programs. Our poll also shows that most Americans think that Saddam still has WMD, and that he had something to do with 9-11," he added. "Have these liberal media pollsters forgotten that 9-11 changed everything?" asked a senior editor at *The Weekly Standard.* The senior editor asked not to be named for this article, but he also added these words, "These liberal media pollsters love to show President Bush's poll numbers sliding downward. The liberal media pollsters hate this war and they hate President Bush, his wife, dog, and his two drunk daughters. . . . Basically they hate America!"

Vice President Dick Cheney, who was at an undisclosed location for security reasons, had this to say, "These people hate America and they have forgotten 9-11. Saddam was and still is, a growing threat, and these people—these liberal pollsters—have nothing better to do than to show President Bush's low poll numbers."

CONCLUSIVE EVIDENCE OF DAVE CULLEN'S EXISTENCE

October 15, 2004

http://blogs.salon.com/0001137

A JOURNALISTIC WAKEUP CALL!—
Jon Stewart rips *Crossfire* a new one on *Crossfire*
by Dave Cullen

SOMETHING INCREDIBLE just happened.

[*Crossfire* hosts Paul] Begala and [Tucker] Carlson thought they were going to have a fun, bubbly lite show, featuring the clown from *The Daily Show*. Jon Stewart sat there and called them hacks to their faces, told them this kind of pathetic journalism is horrible for the country, and pleaded with them to stop.

At first they were incredulous, and thought he was joking. He wasn't, and did not let up.

"I watch your show every day. And it kills me. Oh, it's so painful to watch. Because we need what you do. This is such a great opportunity you have here—to actually get politicians off their marketing and strategy."

"Is this really Jon Stewart?" Tucker asked.

"Yeah, it's someone who watches your show and cannot take it anymore. I just can't."

Begala was smart enough to mostly keep his mouth shut. Tucker Carlson got really bitchy, and made a complete fool of himself, by relentlessly comparing *Crossfire* to *The Daily Show*, and saying Stewart panders too.

Jon kept laughing at him, at the idea of comparing a news show to the journalistic standards of a comedy show.

After a heated, double-incredulous exchange about this, Jon finally shouted, "You're on CNN! The show that leads into me is puppets making crank phone calls! What is WRONG with you?"

Later, Jon got specific, and challenged them on one of my pet peeves. Immediately after the debates, where do you guys go, he asked. Spin Alley. "Now don't you think that for people watching at home, that's kind of a drag? That you're literally walking to a place called deception lane?"

God, thank you Jon Stewart. That's my reaction every time. Why on earth would I want to watch a bunch of people lie, now? For either side? How pointless is that? Either figure out something else to do, or return us to regular programming.

If they had any journalistic integrity, they wouldn't be putting any of that shit on.

What was amazing about this whole thing was that he rips them up on his show all the time, but this time he went on their show, in front of their audience, and called them on what a disgrace they are.

Pretty potent. At least it felt that way watching. And so liberating, to hear a guest turn to them and say exactly what I had always fantasized about a guest saying to them.

Now here's the thing. I don't think Jon's intended audience was just Paul and Tucker. He was talking to all of us in this business. He's been talking about it for quite awhile now, but this was his boldest move yet.

Will the media ever pick up this topic and have a serious discussion and do anything? The hand-wringing I have heard from the media is typically 90% denial. We still don't get why most of the country despises us. What will it take? Will this make a ripple? Stay tuned.[1]

Notes for "A JOURNALISTIC WAKEUP CALL!—
Jon Stewart rips Crossfire a new one on Crossfire"

1. CNN officials announced in January 2005 that *Crossfire* was being canceled. The last segment of the show aired on June 3, 2005, according to the entry "Crossfire (TV Series)," in the online encyclopedia *Wikipedia,* http://en.wikipedia.org/wiki/Crossfire_(television) accessed on April 26, 2006.

CROOKED TIMBER

June 28, 2005

www.crookedtimber.org

Freedom of the press is great if you own one*
by John Quiggin

THE US SUPREME COURT HAS DECLINED to hear a case in which journalists have appealed against a ruling that they should either reveal anonymous sources or go to jail. A noteworthy feature of the *NY Times* treatment of the story is the presentation of the issue in terms of whether journalists are entitled to special protection not available to bloggers. At the end of the story Rodney A. Smolla, dean of the University of Richmond School of Law is quoted as follows:

> The federal judiciary, from the Supreme Court down, has grown very skeptical of any claim that the institutional press is deserving of First Amendment protection over and above those of ordinary citizens . . . The rise of the Inter-

> net and blogger culture may have contributed
> to that. It makes it more difficult to draw lines
> between the traditional professional press and
> those who disseminate information from their
> home computers.

The failure of journalists to establish a special exemption raises the more general question of whether and when people should be compelled to reveal details of their private conversations. If constitutional limits are to be imposed on such questioning, it may be better to derive them from the right to privacy in general rather than the specific claims of the press. Alternatively, and perhaps preferably, it might be better for the legislature to provide a public interest exemption of some kind. On the same topic, I was going to respond to this piece by Margaret Simons about bloggers and journalists but, as often happens, Tim Dunlop has written exactly what I would have said, only better.[1]

* And nowadays everyone does.

Notes for "Freedom of the press is great if you own one*"

1. Tim Dunlop, "If you're a hammer, everything looks like a nail," June 27, 2005, *The Road to Surfdom* web site (http://www.roadtosurfdom .com/archives/2005/06/if_youre_a_hamm.html) accessed on May 29, 2006. In a piece Margaret Simons wrote for *The Age*, she characterized blogs and bloggers as instruments of opinion, not reporters of facts. About the journalist/blogger paradigm, Tim Dunlop responds "Yes, the lines are sometimes blurred, and there is an obvious connection between the two activities, but professional journalists could save themselves a lot of heartache by not working from the blogger=journalist paradigm. The alternative that I've suggested is the blogger=citizen frame, where a blogger is a person who is just excercising their rights of participation in political and social deliberations. Work from that premise and blogging ceases to be 'second-rate' journalism and becomes something a whole lot more hopeful."

C R O O K E D   T I M B E R

June 8, 2005

www.crookedtimber.org

An open letter to the *New Republic*

by Ted Barlow

TO THE EDITORS of the *New Republic*:

I am a former subscriber to your magazine who has let my subscription lapse. I'm one of the people who periodically receives invitations to resubscribe as an "old friend." I should explain that when I let my subscription lapse, I was simply choking in reading materials and not reacting in horror to your non-left positions. (For what it's worth, my most-read weekly nowadays is *BusinessWeek*.) The *New Republic* is excellent far more often than it's infuriating, and we'd be better off if all journals of political opinion shared your willingness to seriously consider the arguments of the other side. Unfortunately, not all arguments are worthy of serious consideration.

Recently, Amnesty International released its 2005 annual report of human rights violations around the globe. In connection with this report, Irene Khan, the Secretary General, made a wide-ranging speech criticizing the United States, the UN, Western Europe, and the governments of Sudan, Zimbabwe, China, and Russia, among others. In this speech, she made an overheated and historically ignorant comparison of Guantanamo Bay to the Soviet gulags. In response, Bush administration officials joined the ignoble ranks of leaders who have responded to Amnesty International reports of human rights abuses with spin and self-pity. President Bush said, "I'm aware of the Amnesty International report, and it's absurd." Vice-President Cheney said that he didn't take Amnesty seriously, and Donald Rumsfeld called the description "reprehensible." A small army of pundits rushed forward to attack Amnesty International's credibility.

We had a truly remarkable debate. On one hand, we had an organization with a 40-year history of standing up for human rights regardless of borders and ideology, criticizing the United States for holding prisoners without due process and torturing them. Only a fool would deny that this is, in fact, happening. On the other hand, we have an Administration accusing Amnesty International of poor word choice. Your contribution to the debate was a piece criticizing Amnesty for the use of the term "gulag."

I completely understand the objection to the term. After all, the gulags were a vastly larger evil, and a part of a far more sinister and omnipresent system of repression. However, I have to question your priorities. Your magazine supported the war on Iraq on the basis of human rights. (Like the Administration, you used Amnesty's reports of Saddam's tyranny without hesitation in arguing for the war.) Surely human rights abuses performed in our name, by our elected government, deserve scrutiny and criticism, even if such abuses don't approach the depths of Stalin or Saddam. It seems obvious to me that Amnesty doesn't deserve your sneers.

We have seen horrors, great and small, in the past century. There have always been some who have done what they could to oppose them. History will not look kindly on those who made excuses, looked the other way, or told the supporters of justice to keep their damn voices down. I expect no better from the alleluia chorus of movement conservatives. Too many have shown that their interest in human rights ends when it ceases to be a useful club against domestic opponents. But I expect more from the *New Republic*.

As I mentioned, I'm frequently invited to resubscribe to your magazine. I see that a digital subscription to the New Republic can be had for $29.95. I'm not going to buy one. Instead, I'm going to send that money to Amnesty International, who have done more for human rights than perhaps any volunteer organization existing. And I'm going to encourage my readers to do the same thing.

Sincerely,

Ted Barlow

P.S. You can imagine a world in which the term "gulag" had not been used in that speech. In that world, do you imagine that the Amnesty report would have set off a serious effort on the part of the Bush Administration to correct its abuses? Or do you think that they would find another excuse—any excuse—to belittle and ignore the report? The question answers itself, doesn't it?

L E F T   I   O N   T H E   N E W S

March 30, 2005

www.lefti.blogspot.com

Looking for real information?
Try non-corporate media

by Eli Stephens

WHILE THE CORPORATE MEDIA are almost literally in "all-Schiavo, all the time"[1] mode, there is lots going on in the world. Why should you listen to (or read) non-corporate media, like Pacifica Radio's *Flashpoints* show? Consider today. The corporate press *did report* on the release of a memo from Lt. Gen. Ricardo Sanchez approving torture (of course you won't find that word in the corporate press). If you dug a little deeper, and *turned to the blogs*, you would have learned an important additional fact, which is that this memo directly contradicted Sanchez's testimony to Congress in which he denied ever approving such measures (thus making him guilty of perjury, lying to Congress, and probably multiple other offenses aside from aiding and abetting torture). But only if you were listening to tonight's *Flashpoints* would you have been reminded that the release of this memo is part of a *civil lawsuit filed by the ACLU* against Sanchez and Donald Rumsfeld, and gotten to hear a long interview with the *lead attorney in that lawsuit*, Lucas Guttentag, and heard him discussing the memo and its implications for the lawsuit. Earlier this month, *Left I on the News* discussed the case of Nicaraguan revolutionary Dora Maria Tellez, and the sparse (to put it mildly) coverage in the press of the U.S. government's denial of a visa for her to teach at Harvard on the grounds that she

CROOKED TIMBER

"Priorities" by Ted Barlow
www.crookedtimber.org
April 22, 2004

AT 10:31 CENTRAL TIME, here's the top news on the top news web sites:

- MSNBC: Trains Crash, Explode
- CBS News: Heavy Toll In N. Korea Train Crash
- FOX News: Report: Thousands Hurt, Killed in N. Korea Crash
- CNN: Michael Jackson indicted
- ABC: Michael Jackson facing trial

The stories on the crash are reporting as many as 3000 dead or injured. Meanwhile, CNN and ABC have the story in sidebars. These are not good priorities, my friend.
UPDATE: At 10:55, Michael Jackson is still the top story at both CNN and ABC.
UPDATE: 11:25. CNN's top story is now the crash, while ABC's is still Michael Jackson.

was a terrorist. But tonight, on *Flashpoints*, you could have heard an interview with Tellez herself, speaking by phone from Managua, discussing the denial, the state of things in Nicaragua today, and so on.

Your chances of ever seeing Guttentag or Tellez on any corporate media talk or news show? Zero.

Want to know what's happening in Haiti? If you read or listen to the corporate media, it would seem the answer is nothing; I've seen or read literally not a word about Haiti in ages. But in fact, as you could hear *live* on *Flashpoints* on Monday, there was an assassination attempt against leading Haitian pro-democracy activist and liberation theologist, Father Jean Juste. On Tuesday, U.N. forces opened fire on peaceful demonstrators. Where could you learn about these developments? Only on *Flashpoints*. Certainly not from the corporate media, even from the "serious" news shows like Aaron Brown's *Newsnight* on CNN or from the "serious" newspapers like the *New York Times* or the *Washington Post*.

And the good news? All of the previous (or at least the reasonably recent) broadcasts of the two most important shows, *Flashpoints* and *Democracy Now!*, are available for download.[2]

Notes for "Looking for real information? Try non-corporate media."

1. The reference is to Terri Schiavo, the St. Petersburg, Florida, woman who collapsed at her home in 1990 and remained in a persistent vegetative state until her husband, Michael, won a protracted legal battle to have her feeding tube removed. She died March 31, 2005, despite attempts by President Bush and Republicans in Congress to intervene in the case and keep her alive. Entry "Terri Schiavo" in the online encyclopedia *Wikipedia*, (http://en.wikipedia.org/wiki/Terri_schiavo) accessed on April 26, 2006.

2. *Democracy Now!* is online at http://www.democracynow.org. *Flashpoints* is online at http://www.flashpoints.net.

THE HUFFINGTON POST
August 22, 2005
www.huffingtonpost.com

Sheehan Breakthroughs, Unbridgeable Divides, and Taboos Unbroken
by David Swanson

THE WASHINGTON POST ON SUNDAY wondered out loud whether Cindy Sheehan might be a "catalyst for a muscular antiwar movement." In translation, this is an assertion that Cindy Sheehan has already become an accepted reason for the corporate media to finally acknowledge the existence of, and consequently help to build, the antiwar movement.

There has, of course, been a major antiwar movement longer than there has been a war. And Cindy Sheehan has been speaking eloquently at antiwar events for many months. What has changed is primarily the media.

A web site called *Blue Oregon* noticed this Saturday and wrote: "the *Oregonian* appears to be using Cindy Sheehan as cover to mention the lies upon which the war was justified." Yes, the Oregonian used the L word:

> The misty scrim that obscured our view of the war—wishful thinking, distortions, outright lies—is rapidly dissolving. Americans increasingly see the war as it is, and know it's going badly. Little wonder that when a gold-star mother parks herself inconsolably in Crawford, Texas, asking hard questions and spurning glib answers, she strikes a nerve.

But it's not been two months since the media, still refusing to call lies lies, was pretending that evidence of lies (like the

Downing Street Memos) was "old news." Now, it's new news, thanks to Cindy. And thanks, also, to the polls, which show public opinion of the war sinking very low. But, most of the thanks goes to the Cindy Sheehan media phenomenon. The media should not base its coverage of presidential lies on public opinion that has managed to form despite the media's silence. And, in fact, comparison with other issues suggests it really doesn't; in many cases strong public opinion is not enough to generate coverage.

When Cindy became a story, many antiwar activists put in hundreds of hours debating and strategizing how to make the "message" focus on lots of families who lost kids in the war and want it to end, rather than just one mother. But for all the framing and messaging attempts, non-reporters (other than Cindy) had very little control over what happened with this story.

Then, when Cindy left to visit her ailing mother, some worried that the media, notoriously unable to cover a movement, would drop the ball and move on to celebrities or sex in some other town. The greatest measure of what Cindy has done is that this has not happened. Cindy has not only left behind her in Crawford and around the country a growing and inspired movement, but she has left behind an ongoing news story about the movement.

On Friday, a Reuters article began: "Supporters of antiwar protester Cindy Sheehan on Friday vowed to stay near U.S. President George W. Bush's Texas ranch in her absence. [. . .]" And the Associated Press's article began: "Although their leader had just departed because of a family emergency, antiwar demonstrators here didn't miss a beat, marching closer to President Bush's ranch to deliver handwritten letters."

The *Rocky Mountain News* on Saturday began an article with the headline "Coloradans to join war protest camp near Bush's ranch," and this opening paragraph: "Karen Trietsch squatted in her living room Friday, finishing the lettering on her neon-pink sign that proclaimed: 'Bush lies, Thousands die.' 'We can no longer view this war as a Nintendo game on CNN,' said Trietsch, 37, who leaves today for Crawford, Texas, with more than a dozen friends."

Of course, people have made similar remarks since before the war started, but they haven't been in lead paragraphs.

The movement has a lot of work to do, and as plans are formalized this week for events in Washington on September 24, 25, and 26, we will see how well it is done. And, of course, the media has very far to go. For one thing, it still gives disproportionate coverage to supporters of the war.

However, there still are supporters of the war in considerable numbers around the country. And there appears at first glance to be an unbridgeable divide between them and us. An AP story from Crawford on Saturday began: "[A] patriotic camp with a 'God Bless Our President!' banner sprung up downtown Saturday, countering the antiwar demonstration started by a fallen soldier's mother two weeks ago near President Bush's ranch. The camp is named 'Fort Qualls,' in memory of Marine Lance Cpl. Louis Wayne Qualls, 20, who died in Iraq last fall. 'If I have to sacrifice my whole family for the sake of our country and world, other countries that want freedom, I'll do that,' said the soldier's father, Gary Qualls, a friend of the local business owner who started the pro-Bush camp. He said his 16-year-old son now wants to enlist, and he supports that decision."

Opponents of the war recoil from this in horror. "God Bless Our President" is a little too theocratic for most of us. A man sacrificing his family is a little too patriarchic for us. (How about leaving it up to the wife and kids to decide whether to sacrifice themselves?) But the big divide here is not one of values or patriotism or courage or malice or racism or empire. The big divide here is between those who believe the war was based on good reasons and those who believe it was based on blatant lies that have been extensively documented. I'd sacrifice my life for the sake of the world. Many people would. But I believe this war is driven by imperialism propped up on fearmongering falsehoods. Gary Qualls would probably insist on protecting his family from being slaughtered to enrich an oligarchy that plays him for a fool. But he believes the war is protecting his family and everyone else's, or at least everyone else he knows and thinks about.

I don't want to discount self-deception. Those who want to support a war will turn a blind eye to exposure of the lies that launched it, just as those who oppose a war will be more tempted to cook up wacky theories about its architects that pile imaginary treasonous plotting on top of the solid case already established. But it does seem to me that the most effective way to change opinion about this war is to educate people about the evidence that the war was launched on the basis of lies.

Public opinion polls show a majority believing that Bush lied about the reasons for the war—and a near majority wanting impeachment proceedings begun. They also show a growing percentage of Americans wanting to end the war, and another large slice of the public wanting a gradual withdrawal begun. These numbers—belief that Bush lied and belief that the war should end—have risen together, the former staying ahead of the latter.

But here the media has played another trick on us. The desire to end the war, while lower in the media's own polls, has become a respectable position in the media's news stories. Meanwhile the belief that the president lied about the war and should be impeached for it, while stronger in the media's own polls, has been almost taboo in news stories. Certainly the I word is completely forbidden in public (that is, corporate controlled) discourse.

And this way of thinking has been accepted thoughtlessly by most Democrats in Congress. While 58 percent of Democrats favor impeachment (Zogby), most progressive Democratic congress members are afraid of the idea. They and their staff members recite the same mantra endlessly: "That would allow the Republicans to attack us." If you don't believe me, call up your congress member. Even call up some of the most progressive members of congress just for kicks. Ask them why in the world they haven't introduced articles of impeachment. They will say the following words: "That would allow the Republicans to attack us."

But what could be better for a Democrat than to be attacked by Republicans over this war? This war is going to drag its supporters down, and any remaining faith in our governmental system along with them, unless an antiwar party develops.

Democrats say they can't attempt things because they are in the minority. But if they do not attempt things that people want, they will stay in the minority.

The case for impeachment is overwhelming. The evidence is compiled at www.afterdowningstreet.org. The congress member who speaks up first will be the hero of a muscular antiwar movement.

THE HUFFINGTON POST

September 15, 2005

www.huffingtonpost.com

Return of the Media

by Josh Silver

MEDIA COVERAGE OF Hurricane Katrina has caused many to marvel at a rare event: Corporate media diverging from White House talking points, criticizing the administration, and bypassing the Karl Rove spin machine. Unlike Iraq coverage, we're seeing the real, graphic and disturbing realities. But the real story is not how good press coverage of Katrina has been: It is the abysmal state of the media to which it's being compared.

There are several media issues on the docket in Washington this fall that will have a profound impact on whether the media will get better or worse.

- **Media Ownership:** Most major media outlets are already owned by a handful of massive corporations whose only concern is the bottom line. FCC Chairman Kevin Martin—under tremendous pressure from media corporations and their friends at the White House—is expected to begin the process of lifting ownership caps that prevent daily newspapers from owning radio and TV stations in the same market and vice versa. These are the same rules Michael Powell pushed in 2003—prompting millions of calls to Congress and the FCC. Martin is hoping to sneak them in quietly before the general public starts paying attention.

- **Public Broadcasting:** The United States provides less funding for public broadcasting than any other developed nation (per capita). Without good public service media, all we'd have left are the commercial media that provide a profoundly narrow range of debate. We've seen the virtual elimination of investigative journalism (into substantive political issues, not the celebrity of the month), rampant commercialism, and an ever-cozier relationship between government, media and corporate elites. Yet this summer the House voted to slash nearly half of the budget for public broadcasting—which was already being attacked from the right for its alleged "liberal bias." Huge public backlash pushed the House to restore some of the money and convinced the Senate to move a bill with full funding. The two versions soon will be reconciled. But don't be surprised if the Republicans try to cut funding again, citing the huge cost of cleaning up after Katrina.

- **Broadband over the Public Airwaves:** Congress will decide whether to provide Americans with a chance at affordable broadband. Using a slice of the public airwaves being returned to the government as part of the digital television transition, legislators could designate the people's airwaves to support high-speed, wireless Internet. This is about the future of communications in America, as TV, radio and telephones will soon be all delivered to your home via a broadband connection. Opening the airwaves to low-cost Internet access would be a huge boon to consumers; most people can't afford broadband (65% of Americans don't have it). But Congress has competing priorities. They want to auction off your spectrum to pay for war and tax cuts for the rich, leaving us stuck with the corrupt system we currently enjoy: duopoly control of Internet access by cable and telephone companies that charge high prices for slow connection speeds. What passes for "broadband" here is 100 times slower than what they're rolling out in Japan and South Korea. The United States is now ranked 16th in the world in broadband penetration, having slipped from fifth when Bush took office.

If you want better media, you need better media policy. So keep an eye on these crucial media policy debates and weigh in as they play out this fall. Just don't count on the corporate media to tell you what's going on.

C O M M O N   D R E A M S
May 22, 2005
www.commondreams

Why We Need a Media and Democracy Act
by Danny Schechter

THE NATIONAL CONFERENCE for Media Reform held last week in St. Louis was a smashing success in generating the momentum that the organizers from Free Press hoped for. Bill Moyers' powerful sermon of a speech during the closing session on Sunday morning was aired on C-SPAN and hurtled through cyberspace faster than that proverbial speeding bullet.

The threat to PBS was put on the agenda—as it should be—with a powerful challenge to Corporation for Public Broadcasting (CPB) Chairman Kenneth Y. Tomlinson. Tomlinson's big-foot strategy at PBS and NPR is being exposed for what is—a right-wing coup that will, if it is successful, drive what remains of more diverse or outspoken programming off the public airwaves.[1]

That came through very clearly.

What has yet to penetrate the progressive community is a deeper understanding of the structural problem here, and the institutional stagnation that PBS has suffered from for years. Unmentioned at the conference was the fact that it was Bill Clinton—not Attila the Hun or Bill O'Reilly—who appointed Tomlinson and, for that matter, [FCC chairman] Michael Powell.

As a TV producer with years of experience producing programming for the PBS that we are now trying to save, I can tell you how flawed the system has been, how timid, and how difficult to work with.

But I won't.

Suffice it to say, anything less than reinventing PBS and imbuing it with a new more courageous spirit and mission will not have the desired effect.

I know. I've been there and done that.

We all like Big Bird, but I am not sure how many adults will go to the mattresses for him. (Well, maybe for Miss Piggy!)

Remember, too, it was the Clinton administration that supported the Telecommunications Act of 1996 with the deluded expectation that consumers would benefit by breaking up media monopolies to achieve more competition.

What we got instead was more media concentration.

What was not appreciated then was how powerful media power is. We have to recognize that the media industries have shoveled oodles of moolah into political campaigns on both sides of the aisle. They are bipartisan and equal-opportunity power brokers.

They are about their bottom line, not advancing democracy.

So, the media problem is not at its heart a partisan one—it's about interests, not issues.

Reforms can't be based on slogans because they have to try to transform structures. As one critic of half-way incremental reformism put it in a newspaper circulated at the conference, we don't want to end up "painting lipstick on the pig."

This is why I believe we need a comprehensive approach, an umbrella strategy that can translate what we really want into a legislative package that many different constituencies can sign onto with the principle that unity is better than disunity, à la the Contract for America. (Note how Hillary Clinton and Newt Gingrich are now best buddies.)

My idea: A Media and Democracy Act to package proposals for an anti-trust program to break up media monopolies; a funding strategy for public broadcasting and the independent producing community (perhaps financed with a tax on advertising); reinstatement of an updated fairness doctrine; free broadcasts for political debate across the spectrum; limits on advertising and monitoring for honesty and accuracy; guarantees for media freedom in the public interest; media literacy education in our schools; provisions for free wireless; media training and access centers; more support for media arts, etc.

This list is endless. No one group has the clout to put its priorities on the agenda without support from others, so why not make everyone a stakeholder in the process? Politics is the art of compromise. That's why a Media and Democracy Act that incorporates all these concerns can have appeal across the partisan divides of politics as well as the political divides within the media and democracy movement.

It is not my job to write the Act. That work can be done by

media reform advocates and by members of Congress and their staffs who know the arcane world of legislation. All I know—or remember—is a chart I first saw in elementary school on "How A Bill Becomes A Law." As I recall, it made no reference to the power of lobbyists, lawyers and snake-oil salesmen on K Street.

One purpose of such an Act is not to expect to prevail the first time out, but to show what is needed and is possible, how government policy shapes the regulatory framework, and how national priorities and funding could be used to make a media system that can truly serve the public interest and inform our democracy.

A Media and Democracy Act is an idea that can help move this movement. It underscores the importance of working together to make media matter and to show a diverse range of interest groups that we can win if we work together.

It's an idea whose time is coming.

I would prefer for it to happen in our lifetimes.

Notes for "Why We Need a Media and Democracy Act"
1. Facing ethics violation charges, Ken Tomlinson resigned from the CPB board in November 2005. He was charged with using agency money to hire consultants and lobbyists without notifying the agency's board, hiring Republican National Committee co-chairman Patricia de Stacy Harrison as CPB's chief executive, and allowing White House influence in his hiring of two in-house ombudsmen to critique news programs on NPR and PBS. Among his many transgressions, he commissioned a $10,000 study into Bill Moyers' *Now with Bill Moyers* to return evidence of liberal bias on the program. As chairman of the Broadcasting Board of Governors (a government agency overseeing Voice of America and other services), he is under investigation for misusing State Department funds and running his horse business from his government office.

BUZZMACHINE

November 24, 2004

www.buzzmachine.com

How to Explode TV News in Four Easy Steps

by Jeff Jarvis

TRY THIS:

1. Slice.

Cut up your shows into stories and put them all online.

After you air a story, it's fishwrap. Nobody can see it. If they missed it, well, that's tough for them. Is that any way to treat your public? Well, you don't have to anymore.

You should put up every story you do—and not just as a stream but as files that the people can distribute on their own.

You can still make money on this—in fact, you'll make new money: Put ads on the video; track those ads; and tack on a Creative Commons license that says people can distribute the video but cannnot muck with it. And you'll find something magical will happen: Your audience will market your product for you and distribute it for you and it won't cost you anything more. It's free money, damnit. Tell that to your stockholders.

And while you're at it, take your script for the segment and associate it with the video as meta data (that is, post it on a blog with a link to the video) so people can find your stories on search engines and then watch them.

This means that people who really *want* to see your stories and are interested in them can now do so. We're no longer captive to your schedule and your selection; we can watch what interests us. We are in control.

The result: You will get a more interested and involved audience. You will get a bigger audience. You will get more people who will like what you do and start watching your old-fashioned shows. You will benefit. We will benefit.

If you really care about informing the public—which, of course, you do—then this is the first step to doing it a new and better way.

2. Add.

You have more material for every story you do: I've seen how much goes into a 3-minute piece and how much is left out.

Now in most cases, I do think that stuff that's cut is extraneous to most people.

You're right to edit and package. Keep it up.

And in the early days of online when news people thought this medium was all about getting more time to tell longer stories with more stuff and another chance to show off cute writing, I screamed in protest: No, your stories are already too long anyway. Find the nearest period!

But for those who are intensely interested in a story or who want to look deeper into what we say, why not put up all the rest of your material? Why throw it away? Put up entire interviews and do it in chunks so people link directly to one piece or another and, in essence, put up their own remixes. Show the world your great reporting.

If you're doing your job right, this will help your credibility and reputation, for most people will see that you really did pick the right stuff and did tell the story well.

More important, you enable people who need more information to get it. And that is our job, isn't it?

3. Link.

It's as simple as that: Link outside of your own echo chamber of a newsroom. Link to your competitors and show what they did on stories—stories you did better, stories you didn't do. Do not assume we are your captive. Assume we are smart and want to be informed and want to find the best reports we can. Also assume that we are a thinking public and we want to see and hear different perspectives on a story so we can decide what we think. So help us. We'll appreciate it.

Link to your competitors. It will be good for you. It will make you want to do better jobs on stories than they do.

4. Listen.

Listen to the people you used to call your audience but should see as your equals.

The next time bloggers suggest a fact of yours may be wrong, CBS, listen to them. Quote them. Look into what they say. Thank them. Learn your lesson, huh?

And it's not just about fact-checking your ass. It's about knowing that your former viewers have something valuable to say. At first, it's just about quoting their words.

But you know that it won't be very long before we're all equipped with cameras and we'll all be witnesses to our 15 minutes of news. The wise news organization will create an easy way to collect and remix and redistribute all that. Wouldn't you like to have eyewitness video from the heart of a new story?

Recognize that anyone can be a reporter. Anyone who sees and reports news is a reporter. So widen your world. Listen. Quote. Make your public a star alongside your anchors.

When you've done all that, you've turned news into a conversation.

You've turned the spotlight away from the anchor—the mere personality who got you in trouble—and you turn it onto the news itself, where it belongs.

You've engaged the people you used to call your viewers, who used to just sit there but have since started walking away, into the news.

You've made anchors what they should be: supporting players, second bananas. (And you've saved yourself a helluva lot of money along the way.)

And you've informed the public. Isn't that what news is about instead of an anchor's fame?

POYNTERONLINE

September 2, 2005

www.poynter.org

Ethical Questions About Covering Katrina
by Kelly McBride

OVER THE NEXT DAYS and weeks newsrooms are going to face ethical challenges every day, in every story out of New Orleans. Here are a handful of challenges and some thoughts about working through them.

Bodies—Many newsrooms have policies that prevent displaying pictures of dead bodies. Yet the bodies are a big part of this story. There is news in the way people are dying, the places they are dying and what is happening to their bodies.

Rigid rules, apart from journalistic values, undermine the truth. Now is the time for newsrooms to remember their primary roles as truth-tellers and watchdogs. That may mean searching for ways to tell the story of the bodies in words and in photos. The story and photo that ran in many papers and on many Web sites (including Poynter's *St. Petersburg Times)* on Wednesday told the story of Evelyn Turner. Her husband died during the hurricane, and she floated his body to City Hall trying to find a place for him. In the photo, the grieving Turner in the forefront, the shrouded body in the background. The story and caption provided context and treated Turner and her husband with respect. Telling the truth about the bodies may be the hardest challenge editors face in the coming days.

Safety—Keeping journalists safe in New Orleans could prove more difficult than keeping them safe in Iraq or Afghanistan. Newsrooms need to be sure journalists have access to resources, an escape route, a support team and good insurance. That means having people outside the most dangerous geographic zones offering support. It might mean paying for security, the way journalists do in other war zones. It certainly means sending in journalists with experience. This might be the first domestic disaster where war correspondents are the most qualified journalists to tell the story.

When to help—Although journalists are often cautioned to not intervene, it's impossible in the face of so much suffering to avoid giving away your water and Power Bars. With the need so vast and the people so desperate, the best strategies are those that allow the journalist to gather the stories, get the stories out and avoid becoming a distraction or creating more danger. Broadcasting the suffering of one could ultimately alleviate the suffering of thousands. But journalists entering the devastation need to think ahead about what they'll do.

When to send staff and when to send more staff—The decision to devote resources to this disaster is immense. For many editors and news directors in areas not affected by Katrina, the key is a local angle, like following a group of hometown volunteers. More important is to tell stories no one else is telling. This is a saga, not a news event. There are millions of untold stories. If you send a crew, do it for the right reasons.

Add to the historic narrative, rather than duplicating the efforts of others. Be a watchdog. Ask the hard questions. Who is in charge? How did this become so drastic? Why hasn't help arrived sooner? Many news reports describe what resources are on the way. Few say why it's taking so long.

Ultimately, telling this story will require courage. Courage to be among the desperate. Courage to spend the money and time. Courage to challenge the powerful. Courage to stay with the story when the immediate crisis is past. Courage to look at our leaders and, ultimately, ourselves, and ask: How did we let this get so bad?

CONSORTIUMNEWS.COM

April 29, 2005

www.consortiumnews.com

The Left's Media Miscalculation

by Robert Parry

TO UNDERSTAND HOW the United States got into today's political predicament—where even fundamental principles like the separation of church and state are under attack—one has to look back at strategic choices made by the Right and the Left three decades ago.

In the mid-1970s, after the U.S. defeat in Vietnam and President Richard Nixon's resignation over the Watergate scandal, American progressives held the upper-hand on media. Not only had the mainstream press exposed Nixon's dirty tricks and published the Pentagon Papers secrets of the Vietnam War, but a vibrant leftist "underground" press informed and inspired a new generation of citizens.

Besides well-known antiwar magazines, such as *Ramparts*, and investigative outlets, like Seymour Hersh's *Dispatch News*, hundreds of smaller publications had emerged across the country in the late 1960s and early 1970s. Though some quickly disappeared, their influence shocked conservatives who saw the publications as a grave political threat. [For details, see Angus Mackenzie's *Secrets: The CIA's War at Home.*[1]]

Conservatives felt out-muscled on a wide range of public-policy fronts, blaming the media not only for the twin debacles of Watergate and Vietnam but also for contributing to the Right's defeat on issues such as civil rights and the environment.

Fateful Choices

At this key juncture, leaders of the Right and the Left made fateful choices that have shaped today's political world. Though both sides had access to similar amounts of money from wealthy individuals and like-minded foundations, the two sides chose to invest that money in very different ways.

The Right concentrated on gaining control of the information flows in Washington and on building a media infrastructure that would put out a consistent conservative message across the country. As part of this strategy, the Right also funded attack groups to target mainstream journalists who got in the way of the conservative agenda.

The Left largely forsook media in favor of "grassroots organizing." As many of the Left's flagship media outlets foundered, the "progressive community" reorganized under the slogan—"think globally, act locally"—and increasingly put its available money into well-intentioned projects, such as buying endangered wetlands or feeding the poor.

So, while the Right waged what it called "the war of ideas"

and expanded the reach of conservative media to every corner of the nation, the Left trusted that local political action would reenergize American democracy.

Some wealthy progressives also apparently bought into the conservative notion of a "liberal bias" in the media and thus saw no real need to invest significantly in information or to defend embattled journalists under conservative attack. After all, over the years, many mainstream journalists did appear allied with liberal priorities.

In the 1950s, for instance, northern reporters wrote sympathetically about the plight of African-Americans in the Jim Crow South. The anger of white segregationists toward that press coverage was the grievance that sparked the first complaints about media "liberal bias."

In one 1955 case, negative national coverage followed the acquittal of two white men for murdering black teenager Emmett Till, who supposedly had whistled at a white woman. Reacting to the critical reporting on the Till case, angry whites plastered their cars with bumper stickers reading, "Mississippi: The Most Lied About State in the Union."

War Over Journalism

The conservative refrain about "liberal bias" grew in volume as mainstream journalists reported critically about the U.S. military strategy in Vietnam and then exposed President Nixon's spying on his political enemies. The fact that reporters essentially got those stories right didn't spare them from conservative ire.

Progressives apparently trusted that professional journalists would continue standing up to conservative pressure, even in the 1980s, as well-funded right-wing groups targeted individual reporters and Reagan-Bush "public diplomacy" teams went into news bureaus to lobby against troublesome journalists. [For details on this strategy, see Robert Parry's *Secrecy & Privilege: Rise of the Bush Dynasty from Watergate to Iraq*, www.secrecyandprivilege.com.]

As those conservative pressures began to take a toll on reporters at the national level, the progressives still emphasized "grassroots organizing" and focused on more immediate priorities, such as filling gaps in the social safety net opened by Reagan-Bush policies.

With the numbers of homeless swelling and the AIDS epidemic spreading, the idea of diverting money to an information infrastructure seemed coldhearted. After all, the social problems were visible; the significance of the information battle was more theoretical.

In the early 1990s, when I first began approaching major liberal foundations about the need to counter right-wing pressure on journalism (which I had seen first-hand at the Associated Press and *Newsweek*), I received dismissive or bemused responses. One foundation executive smiled and said, "we don't *do* media." Another foundation simply barred media proposals outright.

On occasion, when a few center-left foundations did approve media-related grants, they generally went for non-controversial projects, such as polling public attitudes or tracking money in politics, which condemned Democrats and Republicans about equally.

Brock/Coulter

Meanwhile, through the 1990s, the conservatives poured billions of dollars into their media apparatus, which rose like a vertically integrated machine incorporating newspapers, magazines, book publishing, radio stations, TV networks and Internet sites.

Young conservative writers—such as David Brock and Ann Coulter—soon found they could make fortunes working within this structure. Magazine articles by star conservatives earned top dollar. Their books—promoted on conservative talk radio and favorably reviewed in right-wing publications—jumped to the top of the best-seller lists.

While progressives starved freelancers who wrote for left-of-center publications like *The Nation* or *In These Times*, conservatives made sure that writers for the *American Spectator* or the *Wall Street Journal*'s editorial page had plenty of money to dine at Washington's finest restaurants.

(Brock broke away from this right-wing apparatus in the late 1990s and described its inner workings in his book, *Blinded by the Right*.[2] By then, however, Brock had gotten rich writing hit pieces against people who interfered with the conservative agenda, from law professor Anita Hill, who accused Supreme Court Justice Clarence Thomas of sexual harassment, to President Bill Clinton, whose impeachment troubles were touched off by one of Brock's articles in 1993.)

As the 1990s wore on, mainstream journalists adapted to the new media environment by trying not to offend the conservatives. Working journalists knew that the Right could damage or destroy their careers by attaching the "liberal" label. There was no comparable danger from the Left.

So, many Americans journalists—whether consciously or not—protected themselves by being harder on Democrats in the Clinton administration than they were on Republicans during the Reagan-Bush years. Indeed, through much of the 1990s, there was little to distinguish the hostile scandal coverage of Clinton in the *Washington Post* and *The New York Times* from what was appearing in the *New York Post* and the *Washington Times*.

Slamming Gore

The animus toward Clinton then spilled over into Campaign 2000 when the major media—both mainstream and right-wing—jumped all over Al Gore, freely misquoting him and subjecting him to almost unparalleled political ridicule. By contrast, George W. Bush—while viewed as slightly dimwitted—got the benefit of nearly every doubt. [See *Consortiumnews.com*'s "Al Gore v. the Media," www. consortiumnews.com/2000/020100a.html" or "Protecting Bush-Cheney, http://www.consortiumnews.com/2000101500a .html."]

During the Florida recount battle, liberals watched as even the *Washington Post*'s center-left columnist Richard Cohen sided with Bush. There was only muted coverage when conservative activists from Washington staged a riot outside the Miami-Dade canvassing board, and scant mention was made of Bush's phone call to joke with and congratulate the rioters. [See *Consortiumnews.com*'s "Bush's Conspiracy to Riot," http://www. consortiumnews.com/2002/080502a.html.]

Then, once five Republicans on the U.S. Supreme Court blocked a state-court-ordered recount and handed Bush the White House, both mainstream and conservative news outlets acted as if it were their patriotic duty to rally around the legitimacy of the new President. [For more on this phenomenon, see Parry's *Secrecy & Privilege*, http://www.secrecyandprivilege. com.]

The protect-Bush consensus deepened after the September 11, 2001, terror attacks as the national news media—almost across the board—transformed itself into a conveyor belt for White House propaganda. When the Bush administration put out dubious claims about Iraq's supposed weapons of mass destruction, the major newspapers rushed the information into print.

Many of the most egregious WMD stories appeared in the most prestigious establishment newspapers, *The New York Times* and *The Washington Post*. *The New York Times* fronted bogus assertions about the nuclear-weapons capabilities of aluminum tubes that were really for conventional weapons. *Washington Post* editorials reported Bush's allegations about Iraqi WMD as fact, not a point in dispute.

Antiwar protests involving millions of American citizens received largely dismissive coverage. Critics of the administration's WMD claims, such as former weapons inspector Scott Ritter and actor/activist Sean Penn, were ignored or derided. When Al Gore offered thoughtful critiques of Bush's preemptive-war strategy at rallies organized by MoveOn.org, he got savaged in the national media. [See *Consortiumnews.com*'s "Politics of Preemption," www.consortiumnews.com/2002/100802a.html.]

Smart Investment

Over those three decades, by investing smartly in media infrastructure, the Right had succeeded in reversing the media dynamic of the Watergate-Vietnam era. Instead of a tough skeptical press corps challenging war claims on Iraq and exposing political dirty tricks in Florida, most national journalists knew better than to risk losing their careers.

Many on the Left began acknowledging the danger caused by this media imbalance. But even as the Iraq War disaster worsened, the "progressive establishment" continued spurning proposals for building a media counter-infrastructure that could challenge the "group think" of Washington journalism.

One of the new excuses became that the task was too daunting. When proposals were on the table in 2003 for a progressive AM talk radio network, for example, many wealthy liberals shunned the plan as certain to fail, an attitude that nearly became a self-fulfilling prophecy as an under-funded Air America Radio almost crashed and burned on take-off in March 2004.

Later, the argument was that a media infrastructure would take too long to build and that all available resources should go to oust Bush in Election 2004. To that end, hundreds of millions of dollars were poured into voter registration drives and into campaign commercials. But the consequences of the Left's longtime media disarmament continued to plague its preferred policies and candidates.

When the pro-Bush Swift Boat Veterans for Truth sandbagged Kerry over his Vietnam War record, the conservative media infrastructure made the anti-Kerry attacks big news, joined by mainstream outlets such as CNN. But liberals lacked the media capacity to counter the charges.

By the time the major newspapers got around to examining the Swift Boat allegations and judged many to be spurious, Kerry's campaign was in freefall.

Similarly, there was no significant independent media capability to quickly investigate and publicize voting irregularities on Election Day 2004. *Ad hoc* citizens groups and Internet bloggers tried to fill the void but lacked the necessary resources.

Post-Mortem

Once Election 2004 was over, many progressive funders found a new reason to put off action on a media infrastructure. They said they were financially strapped from the campaign.

Though media issues were part of the post-election post-mortem, actual media plans made little progress. The main activities on the Left centered around arranging more conferences on media and holding more discussions, not implementing concrete proposals to actually do journalism and build new outlets.

There also was a new variation on the Left's three-decade-old emphasis on "grassroots organizing." *MoveOn.org* postponed action on media infrastructure in favor of rallying political activists in support of Democratic legislative goals.

When media activist Carolyn Kay presented a comprehensive media reform strategy (http://makethemaccountable.com/caro/Progressive_Media_Strategy.pdf), MoveOn.org's founder Wes Boyd responded with an e-mail on April 24 saying, "Just to be direct and frank, we have no immediate plans to pursue funding for media . . .

> Our efforts are focused on a few big fights right now, because this is the key legislative season. Later in the year and next year I expect there will [be] more time to look further afield.

Kay e-mailed Boyd back, saying, "For five years people have been telling me that in just a couple of months, we'll start addressing the long-term problems. But the day never comes. . . . Today it's Social Security and the filibuster. Tomorrow it will be something else. And in a couple of months it will be something else again. There's never a right time to address the media issue. That's why the right time is now."

Boyd's April 24 e-mail—calling the idea of addressing the nation's media crisis as wandering "afield"—is typical of the views held by many leaders in the "progressive establishment."

There is no sense of urgency about media.

Still, MoveOn's blasé attitude may be even more surprising since the organization emerged as a political force during the media-driven impeachment of President Clinton. It also watched as Gore's MoveOn-sponsored, pre-Iraq-War speeches were trashed by the national news media, reinforcing his decision to forego a second race against Bush.

Indeed, one point many on the Left still fail to appreciate is how much easier it would be to convince a politician to take a courageous stand—as Gore did in those speeches—if the politician didn't have to face such a hostile media reaction. Already the growth of "progressive talk radio"—on the AM dial in more than 50 cities—appears to have boosted the fighting spirit of some congressional Democrats. [See *Consortiumnews.com*'s "Mystery of the Democrats' New Spine," http://www. consortiumnews.com/2005/042605.html.]

Investigative Journalism

At *Consortiumnews.com* over the past year, we have approached more than 100 potential funders about supporting an investigative journalism project modeled after the Vietnam-era *Dispatch News*, where Sy Hersh exposed the My Lai massacre story. Our idea was to hire a team of experienced investigative journalists who would dig into important stories that are receiving little or no attention from the mainstream news media.

While nearly everyone we have approached agrees on the need for this kind of journalism and most praised the plan, no one has yet stepped forward with financial support. Indeed, the expenses of contacting these potential funders—though relatively modest—have put the survival of our decade-old web site at risk.

Which leads to another myth among some on the Left: that

the media problem will somehow solve itself, that the pendulum will swing back when the national crisis gets worse and the conservatives finally go too far.

But there is really no reason to think that some imaginary mechanism will reverse the trends. Indeed, the opposite seems more likely. The gravitational pull of the Right's expanding media galaxy keeps dragging the mainstream press in that direction. Look what's happening at major news outlets from CBS to PBS, all are drifting to the Right.

As the Right keeps plugging away at its media infrastructure, the pervasiveness of the conservative message also continues to recruit more Americans to the fold.

Ironically, the conservative media clout has had the secondary effect of helping the Right's grassroots organizing, especially among Christian fundamentalists. Simultaneously, the progressives' weakness in media has undercut the Left's grassroots organizing because few Americans regularly hear explanations of liberal goals. But they do hear—endlessly—the Right's political storyline.

Many progressives miss this media point when they cite the rise of Christian Right churches as validation of a grassroots organizing strategy. What that analysis leaves out is the fact that the Christian Right originally built its strength through media, particularly the work of televangelists Pat Robertson and Jerry Falwell. What the Right has demonstrated is that media is not the enemy of grassroots organizing but its ally.

Bright Spots & Dangers

Though there have been some recent bright spots for the Left's media—the fledgling progressive talk radio, new techniques for distributing documentaries on DVD, and hard-hitting Internet blogs—there are also more danger signs. As the Left postpones media investments, some struggling progressive news outlets—which could provide the framework for a counter-infrastructure—may be headed toward extinction.

Just as the echo chamber of the Right's infrastructure makes conservative media increasingly profitable, the lack of a Left infrastructure dooms many promising media endeavors to failure.

The hard truth for the Left is that the media imbalance in the United States could very easily get much worse. The difficult answer for the progressive community is to come to grips with this major strategic weakness, apply the Left's organizing talents, and finally make a balanced national media a top priority.

Notes for "The Left's Media Miscalculation"
1. Angus Mackenzie, *Secrets: The CIA's War at Home* (Berkeley: University of California Press, 1997).

2. David Brock, *Blinded by the Right: The Conscience of an Ex-Conservative* (New York: Crown Publishers, Inc. 2002).

EPILOGUE

FOREVER WIRED:

keepers of internet media

Is THIS THE BEST OF TIMES, or is it the worst of times?

At times it feels like the rise of Internet media has given ordinary citizens a voice never before realized in our democracy—even greater, perhaps, than the revolutionary times of the pamphleteers like Thomas Paine.

Then again, at times it feels like the technology of the Internet makes it too easy for governments and corporations to see what we are reading and where our interests lie. Never before have we been so unsure of our ability to retain privacy. And, looming somewhere in the background is the threat that the Internet, like television and radio before it, will become consolidated in the name of efficiency and standards to the point of delivering more narrowly defined, self-censored versions of the truth than we see today.

Enter the keepers of the Internet. In this epilogue, we'll look at four hotspots for the Internet: sites devoted to maintaining freedom of expression on the Internet, media activist sites, sites specializing in media criticism, and some exemplary sites that are particularly good at covering stories missed by big media.

I. Public Policy: A Free and Open Internet
KEY SITES:
Save the Internet: www.savetheinternet.com
Electronic Frontier Foundation (EFF): www.eff.org

TWO OF THE MOST ACTIVE of activist sites address the central issue of maintaining free expression on the Internet. *Save the Internet* focuses on the issue of Net Neutrality. Put simply, Net Neutrality is public policy legislation that prevents telecommunications companies from limiting access to small web sites that are unable to pay for fast-lane access to the Internet backbone, the large collection of high-capacity "pipeline" that transfers data around the Internet. Without Net Neutrality, web sites unable to pay for fast-lane service could become extremely slow, or even completely unavailable.

Founded in 1990, the Electronic Frontier Foundation (EFF) addresses a host of issues related to keeping the Internet free and open, focusing on copyright law and privacy issues. Among the topics listed on its site are anonymity, bloggers' rights, censorship, copyright law, fair use, file-sharing, intellectual property, Internet governance, privacy, spam, surveillance, and the USA PATRIOT Act.

The Internet was born of public policy. The development of the Internet was a publicly-funded project begun in 1957 with the founding of the Advanced Research Projects Agency (ARPA), and only after about 25 years of public financing did it make sense for commercial developers to enter into the picture. When private companies moved in, they relied on public easements to put in the hardware that is the Internet backbone. Moving ahead, maintaining the Internet as we have come to know it is going to be a matter of sound public policy, not a matter of allowing corporations (who stand to benefit from "owning the Internet") to determine how best to serve their most well-heeled clientele. For learning about the issues that will shape the future of the Internet, these two sites are excellent resources.

II. Getting Involved: Media Activism

KEY SITES:

Fairness and Accuracy in Reporting: www.fair.org

Media Matters for America: http://mediamatters.org

Free Press: www.freepress.net

FOR MANY, DIRECT MEDIA ACTIVISM is an abstract idea. News outlets are supposed to report the news, so what are you supposed to do if you don't like it? Create better news?

Two recommended sites for learning how to be a media critic and getting involved are Fairness and Accuracy in Reporting (FAIR) and Media Matters for America.

Fairness and Accuracy in Reporting (FAIR) provides a Media Activist Kit (www.fair.org/index.php?page=119) that helps explain what to look for in good reporting and how to register a complaint about coverage. Here's a useful bit of advice from one of the pages: "Communicating with journalists makes a difference. It does not have to be perfect; not all letters to journalists need to be for publication. Even a one-sentence, handwritten note to a reporter can be helpful." For deeper involvement, there is an impressive list of media contacts with clickable e-mail links and a recommended readings list, along with other important information.

FAIR operates mainly as a media watchdog. Along with

web site updates, they publish *Extra!*, a bimonthly magazine, and broadcast *CounterSpin*, a radio program that runs down weekly highlights, or lowlights rather, of media coverage.

Unlike FAIR, *Media Matters for America* operates strictly on the web. Started in May 2004 by David Brock, who formerly pushed conservative agendas in the media (most famously, he helped to smear Anita Hill in the hearings to approve Clarence Thomas for the Supreme Court), Media Matters is a self-described "progressive research and information center dedicated to comprehensively monitoring, analyzing, and correcting conservative misinformation in the U.S. media." *Media Matters for America* is frequently updated with examples of media coverage that misinforms viewers, listeners, and readers.

Free Press tracks key media issues such as bills moving through Congress and news stories about the media. According to their site, "The Free Press Action Fund is a social welfare organization advocating for changes in public policy that will lead to a more diverse and public service-oriented media system. The Free Press Action Fund uses creative communications to link specific legislative proposals with aggressive field organizing to mobilize people to take action when it is most needed." The site is easy to use and presents strategies and ideas searchable by region or issue.

III. Meta-Media: Critics of News Coverage

KEY SITES:

The Daily Howler: www.dailyhowler.com

The News Hounds: www.newshounds.us

Crooks and Liars: www.crooksandliars.com

Media Bloggers Association: http://mediabloggers.org

THERE IS REALLY NOTHING like Bob Somerby's *The Daily Howler*.

If biting humor and righteous ranting could reform the media, then the date of media reformation could be pegged to April 1, 1998, the day *The Daily Howler* went online. Alas, eight years later, Somerby still pumps out screens and screens of worthy, informative media criticism that at times makes you wonder how one person could devote so much time to collecting material and still have time to write it up. Informing *and* entertaining is one trademark of a good blog, and Somerby's site does both in spades.

In 2004, media criticism hit the big time with filmmaker Robert Greenwald's documentary *Outfoxed: Rupert Murdoch's War on Journalism.* Timed for release before the November election, the movie showed the inner workings of Fox News, and, by extension, cable television news in general. Research was done by volunteers who monitored Fox News 24 hours a day for months on end. Several of those volunteers continue their work on the *News Hounds* site (motto: "We watch FOX so you don't have to"), where updates come almost as rapidly as the news reports themselves—about 10 updates per day. The observations there could be applied to most programming on cable news networks.

A relative newcomer to blogging is John Amato's *Crooks and Liars.* Since February 2005 the site has specialized in collecting pieces of newscast video for play over the Internet. Because it allows visitors to critically view and not just read about media missteps and atrocities, the site has risen very rapidly to become one of the most-visited blogs devoted primarily to covering the media.

For something more sober, Media Bloggers Association offers one-stop shopping for media commentators from across the spectrum.

IV. Death by a Thousand Cuts: The Blogosphere

KEY SITES:

Josh Marshall: www.talkingpointsmemo.com, www.tpmcafe.com,
   http://tpmmuckraker.com
Eschaton: http://atrios.blogspot.com
Instapundit: www.instapundit.com
LewRockwell.com: http://blog.lewrockwell.com

IF THERE IS ONE Internet phenomenon that is changing media directly, it is the blogosphere. Because they are so inexpensive and easy to start up, web logs have been started by millions and millions of people. Of these, merely millions are devoted to politics and news. Naturally, there is no point trying to track down their every influence or list them at length. As a broad statement, political bloggers do not report the news; they act as news editors and write commentary. There are exceptions, of course. As Josh Marshall wrote in a post dated 29 March 2006, there are instances of major media picking up stories originally reported on blogs (http://www.talkingpointsmemo .com/archives/week_2006_03_26.php#008044). In this case, Marshall wrote about an Associated Press story that ran without credit to his *TPMmuckraker.com* site, where the story broke. It is not the norm, but it does happen.

Josh Marshall has in fact built his own mini Internet media empire. Beginning in November 2000 with his blog *Talking Points Memo*, Marshall grew his readership steadily through the years, becoming one of the main sites for following stories in painstaking detail. In May 2005, he launched *TPM Cafe*, a community blog where many issues are addressed by many different writers, all with some particular expertise. There are regular updates on issues such as Foreign Affairs, Economics, Politics, and the Supreme Court.

Between *Talking Points Memo* and *TPM Cafe*, there may be more material posted than anyone wishing to keep informed could possible follow. But in February 2006, *TPMmuckraker .com* came online with its staff of four (Managing Editor Kate Cambor, researcher Ben Craw, and reporter-bloggers Paul Kiel and Justin Rood) to follow and report on stories in great depth. The sophistication of the reporting on *TPMmuckraker.com* and the commentary on *Talking Points Memo* and *TPM Cafe* pose a direct challenge to establishment news media; it's Josh Marshall showing major media what can be accomplished with just a few computers and a small staff.

Two other sites stand out as representatives of the American political spectrum. Duncan Black, blogging as "Atrios" at *Eschaton*, is the prototypical left/liberal independent blogger, and Glenn Reynolds' *Instapundit* is a right/conservative independent blog. Both blogs log well over 100,000 visitors per day, and both sites have extensive lists of links (blogrolls) leading to other sites, many of them like-minded. In fact, if you wanted to survey every leading political blog, you could do it very well by clicking the links at *Instapundit* and *Eschaton*, then clicking the links that appear on those sites. You would end up visiting tens of thousands, if not hundreds of thousands of reasonably well-trafficked political web logs.

Finally, Lew Rockwell's *LewRockwell.com* gives voice to a libertarian point of view. Long pushed to the side in major media as too far outside the mainstream to be taken seriously, libertarian thought is given expression on the Internet, where "alternative" points of view are the mode of the day. More than 40,000 visitors per day read Lew Rockwell's blog.

And Rockwell has a good grasp on why Internet media has such appeal. In a January 2006 interview with Karen Kwiatkowski, Rockwell said, "The Internet has called forth a whole lot of new writers . . . people who never could have gotten published before the Internet. The regular magazines and newspapers would have been closed to them. In my own experience, the *Los Angeles Times* was the biggest medium I ever got published in, and it was a huge deal to get something in there. I mean, you spent weeks not just writing the thing but you were dealing with editors, and you never knew whether it was going to get in or when it was going to appear. And it was a struggle. [. . .] And now, *everybody* can be a writer."

And everybody can be a reader. And everybody can participate in all kinds of ways. Get busy.

10 QUESTIONS
for every candidate and elected official
(formulated by Free Press: www.freepress.net)

THE FOLLOWING LIST of questions is reprinted by permission of Free Press and is available online at www.freepress.net/congress/questions.php.

1) CONSOLIDATION

Do you support setting limits on media consolidation—through antitrust law and ownership protections—to prevent large companies from having too much control over what Americans see, hear and read?

Why to ask this: The United States has seen a massive wave of media consolidation over the past two decades. For example, Time Warner alone—in addition to its cable empire reaching 11 million subscribers—controls over 100 magazines, dozens of television networks and record companies, as well as major publishing, Internet, TV and movie production companies.

2) NONCOMMERCIAL MEDIA

Do you support policies that would increase and preserve funding for public and noncommercial media, and eliminate commercial sponsorship of public radio and TV programs?

Why to ask this: Democratic discourse requires quality sources of information free from advertiser pressure. However, we provide less funding per capita for public broadcasting than most other industrialized countries—by a wide margin.

3) KIDS' MARKETING

Do you support efforts to reduce commercialism and predatory marketing toward children, and to promote noncommercial educational TV programming for young children?

Why to ask this: Our children today are bombarded with advertising. Parents, teachers, and organizations dedicated to children's issues are growing increasingly concerned as evidence mounts connecting media exposure to a variety of health and behavior problems.

4) CABLE RATES

Will you promote consumer choice by setting limits on cable ownership and by supporting policies to encourage the development of competition in cable markets?

Why to ask this: Over the past 5 years, cable rates have risen over 40% nationwide. This is the direct result of government-granted monopolies and lack of competition. The government has stalled on setting reasonable cable ownership limits. Meanwhile, cable companies are increasing their profits as they eliminate communities' ability to negotiate public-interest-oriented cable agreements.

5) INTERNET FREEDOM

Do you support open access rules that keep the Internet free and open, and that protect individual privacy from both government and corporations alike?

Why to ask this: The Internet exploded over the past decade in part because Internet Service Providers were required by law to allow access to all web sites and users without discrimination. Big cable and telephone companies now want to restrict what users and providers can and cannot access, all in the name of profit.

6) CAMPAIGN COVERAGE

Do you support requiring broadcasters to provide significant free airtime for candidates and public debates as a condition of receiving their government-granted licenses?

Why to ask this: The skyrocketing cost of buying ad time is a major reason candidates raise ever-higher sums of campaign money from wealthy special interests. This year, TV broadcasters—who hold licenses to use publicly-owned airwaves, free of charge—will rake in a record-setting $1.47 billion from political ads. At the same time, news coverage of campaigns, especially on radio and television, has plummeted.

7) COMMUNITY MEDIA

Do you support giving more communities the ability to transmit their own local programming through strengthened cable access centers and expanded low-power radio services?

Why to ask this: Many communities find themselves and their concerns misrepresented by major broadcasters. Citizens need to hear their own voices over their own airwaves and on their local cable systems, and the capability exists to fulfill this demand. Legislation is pending that would create thousands of new low-power FM radio licenses. Legislation needs to be strengthened to better support PEG (Public, Educational and Governmental) access on cable as well, and to include access on satellite.

8) MINORITY OWNERSHIP

Do you support providing incentives to increase diversity in media ownership and leadership?

Why to ask this: Minority ownership of media is at a 10-year low, down 14% since 1997. Today, only 4% of radio stations and 1.9% of television stations are minority-owned. And studies show that the glass ceiling for women is firmly in place at communications companies.

9) MEDIA WORKERS

Do you support laws that make it easier for media workers to form trade unions and ensure they are paid for their overtime?

Why to ask this: Media consolidation pressures media workers to abandon their professional values in order to generate maximum short-term profits. Trade unions are especially important in media industries because they serve both to protect the rights of workers and to insulate the media's role in our democracy from economic pressure.

10) COPYRIGHT

Do you support policies that will shorten the terms of copyright and lend balance to the law by allowing fair use for nonprofit and noncommercial purposes?

Why to ask this: Large corporations are buying protection from new competition and technological innovation. No copyrighted work created after 1922 has entered the public domain—an incubator for new ideas—due to legislation extending copyright terms. If laws being considered today had been in effect a few generations ago, consumers might not have access to products such as VCRs and copiers.

BIOGRAPHY

CONTRIBUTORS
in order of appearance

John Nichols (Alternet.org)

John Nichols covers politics for The Nation magazine and is associate editor of *The Capital Times* newspaper in Madison, Wisconsin. He, Robert W. McChesney, and Josh Silver co-founded *Free Press*, the national media reform network. He is the author or co-author of six books on politics an media, including, with McChensey, *Tragedy and Farce: How the American Media Sell Wars, Spin Elections, and Destroy Democracy* (The New Press: 2005).

Greg Palast (Common Dreams)

Greg Palast is author of the *New York Times* bestsellers, *The Best Democracy Money Can Buy* and *Armed Madhouse*, in which you can find an expanded version of "The Lynching of Dan Rather." Palast, whose reports appear on BBC Television and in the *Guardian* newspapers of Britain, is "America's top investigative reporter, yet is persona non grata in his own country's mainstream newsrooms" (*Asia Times*). To see Palast's reports on the Bush draft-dodging story and his other investigative scoops for BBC Television and the *Guardian* of Britain, go to www.GregPalast.com.

Josh Marshall (Talking Points Memo)

Joshua Micah Marshall is the publisher of *Talking Points Memo*, *TPMCafe*, and *TPMmuckraker.com*. He also writes a weekly column for the Capitol Hill newspaper *The Hill*.

His articles on politics, culture and foreign affairs have appeared in numerous magazines and newspapers such as *The American Prospect*, *The Atlantic Monthly*, *The Boston Globe*, *The Financial Times*, *Foreign Affairs*, *The Los Angeles Times*, *The New Republic*, *The New Yorker*, *The New York Post*, *The New York Times*, *Salon* and *Slate*.

He has appeared on CNN, CNBC, C-SPAN, FOX and MSNBC and is a frequent guest on radio stations across the country.

Marshall graduated from Princeton in 1991 and holds a doctorate in American history from Brown. He lives in New York City with his wife Millet and their dog Simon.

J.C. (Media Matters)

J.C.'s commentary appears online at the Media Matters for America (http://mediamatters.org), a progressive media watchdog group.

John Atcheson (Common Dreams)

John Atcheson has written extensively on politics and policy, and his writing has appeared in the *Washington Post*, *The Baltimore Sun*, *The San Jose Mercury News*, *The Memphis Commercial Appeal* and several other papers, as well as various wonk journals. He has over 30 years experience in government and with the nation's premier think tanks.

Eric S. Margolis (Big Eye)

Eric Margolis is a foreign correspondent, defense analyst and columnist. He is the author of *War at The Top of The World: The Struggle for Afghanistan, Kashmir, and Tibet*. He is the *Toronto Sun*'s contributing foreign editor and a contributing editor at *American Conservative Magazine*.

Bob Somerby (Daily Howler)

Bob Somerby is best known in Washington as one of the city's most popular topical comedians. *National Journal's* Hotline recently called him "one of the top political/consumer comedians of our time."

But years before he began his career as a topical humorist, Bob Somerby, editor of *The Daily Howler*, was an op-ed writer in *The Baltimore Sun*, writing on a variety of political and social issues.

After graduating from Harvard in 1969, Somerby came to Baltimore as a fifth grade teacher in the Baltimore City Public Schools. His first articles in *The Sun*, in 1978, dealt with issues of educational testing.

He has consulted for a variety of network news shows on issues of educational testing. He has written articles for *The Sun* on issues ranging from the outrageous treatment of poor Nancy Kerrigan right on through Medicare funding.

Somerby has appeared on a variety of national TV shows, including *Politically Incorrect* with Bill Maher and *Equal Time* with Mary Matalin and Dee Dee Myers. He once followed Robert Bork on Judith Regan's Fox program. Now, that's a grim opening act!

Christopher Bollyn (American Free Press)

Christopher Bollyn is an investigative journalist working for the *American Free Press*

Jay Rosen (PressThink)

Jay Rosen teaches Journalism at New York University, where he has been on the faculty since 1986.

He is author of *PressThink*, a weblog about journalism and its ordeals (www.pressthink.org), online since September 2003. In June 2005, *PressThink* won the Reporters Without Borders 2005 Freedom Blog award for outstanding defense of free expression. He also blogs at *The Huffington Post*.

Rosen is author of *What Are Journalists For?* (Yale University Press), about the rise of the civic journalism movement. Rosen wrote and spoke frequently about civic journalism (also called public journalism) over a ten-year period, 1989–99. From 1993 to 1997 he was the director of the Project on Public Life and the Press, funded by the Knight Foundation.

As a press critic and reviewer, he has appeared in numerous magazines and national newspapers, including *The Nation*, *Columbia Journalism Review*, the *Chronicle of Higher Education*, the *New York Times*, the *Washington Post*, the *Los Angeles Times*, *Newsday* and others. Online he has written for *Salon.com*, *TomPaine.com* and *Poynter.org*. In 1990 he and Neil Postman hosted a radio show on WBAI in New York called *The Zeitgeist Hour*.

David Sirota (Pop Matters)

David Sirota is a writer political strategist, and author of *Hostile Takeover* (Crown, May 2006). He is the co-chairperson of the Progressive Legislative Action Network (PLAN), and a Senior Editor at *In These Times* magazine. He is also a twice-a-week guest on the *Al Franken Show*, and a bi-weekly contributor to *The Nation* magazine.

Ted Barlow (Crooked Timber)

Ted Barlow is a contributor to the *Crooked Timber* blog. He lives in Houston, TX with his fiancee and their crime-fighting dog.

Sheldon Drobny (The Huffington Post)

Sheldon Drobny was the co-founder of Air America Radio and is the Chairman and Managing Director of Paradigm Group II, a venture capital firm specializing in socially responsible businesses.

Russ Baker (TomPaine)

Russ Baker is an award-winning investigative reporter and essayist, and a contributing editor to *TomPaine.com*. He is the founder of the *Real News Project* (www.realnews.org), a nonprofit investigative reporting team and news outlet. His own web site and blog can be found at www.russbaker.com.

The Cranky Media Guy (Cranky Media Guy)

Bob Pagani was born and raised in New York City. Thanks largely to many jobs as a radio morning show DJ and talk show host, he now lives in Oregon, his eighth state.

As an on-air personality and media hoaxer, often in conjunction with America's best-known hoaxer, Alan Abel, Bob has been seen on *The Today Show*, *Good Morning America*, and *Oprah*, among many other national and local TV shows. He has also been featured in *Time*, *Life*, and *People* magazines as well as most of the major newspapers in America. Most recently, in February 2006, Bob fooled the TV networks and national press into believing he was the winner of America's largest-ever Powerball lottery in Lincoln, Nebraska.

Bob's web site, Cranky Media Guy (crankymediaguy.com) was a blog before the word "blog" was invented. Cranky Media Guy 2.0 is currently in development.

Bob is available to develop media hoaxes that get attention for you or your business. He can be reached at bronxbob@gmail.com.

Bryan Zepp Jamieson (Pundit Pap)

Zepp was born in Ottawa, Ontario, and spent his formative years living in various parts of Canada from Halifax to Victoria, and then the UK, South Africa, and Australia before moving to the United States, where he has lived for 40 years. Aside from writing, his interests include hiking, raising dogs and cats, and making computers jump through hoops. His wife of 25 years edits his copy, and bravely attempts to make him sound coherent. Zepp lives on Mount Shasta.

Robert Parry (consortiumnews.com)

Robert Parry broke many of the Iran-Contra stories in the 1980s for the Associated Press and *Newsweek*. He is author of *Secrecy & Privilege: Rise of the Bush Dynasty from Watergate to Iraq* (The Media Consortium, 2004).

RepublicanPress.com Staff (RepublicanPress)

From the authors: "The creators/writers of RepublicanPress.com are Chris and Jay, two damn good Democrats from Tennessee. We started *RepublicanPress.com* when Pat Robertson, of the 700 Club, came to us in a vision and said that we should either start a

Republican news site, or give him ten thousand dollars. Since we had no money, we decided to create *RepublicanPress.com*. *RepublicanPress.com* is an online magazine devoted to delivering the truth with honor, morals, integrity, and shit like that."

Dave Cullen (Conclusive Evidence of Dave Cullen's Existence)

Dave Cullen has published at *Salon*, *Slate*, *The New York Times* and elsewhere. His upcoming book, *A Lasting Impression on the World: The Definitive Account of Columbine and Its Aftermath* will be published by Dutton in 2007.

John Quiggin (Crooked Timber)

John Quiggin is Australian Research Council Federation Fellow, University of Queensland, Australia. His blog is at http://johnquiggin.com.

Eli Stephens (Left I on the News)

Eli Stephens is proprietor of *Left I on the News*, Press Action Award winner for "Best Media Blog (2005)" and online since 2003.

David Swanson (The Huffington Post)

David Swanson is the Washington Director of Democrats.com and of ImpeachPAC.org. He is co-founder of the AfterDowning Street.org coalition, creator of MeetWithCindy.org, and a board member of Progressive Democrats of America. He serves on the steering committee of the Charlottesville Center for Peace and Justice and on a working group of United for Peace and Justice. He has worked as a newspaper reporter and as a communications director, with jobs including Press Secretary for Dennis Kucinich's 2004 presidential campaign, Media Coordinator for the International Labor Communications Association, and three years as Communications Coordinator for ACORN, the Association of Community Organizations for Reform Now. He serves on the Executive Council of the Washington Baltimore Newspaper Guild. He obtained a Master's degree in philosophy from the University of Virginia in 1997. His web site is www.davidswanson.org.

Josh Silver (The Huffington Post)

Josh Silver founded Free Press with Robert McChesney and John Nichols in 2002. Josh previously served as campaign manager for the successful ballot initiative for Clean Elections in Arizona; director of development for the cultural arm of the Smithsonian Institution in Washington; and director of an international youth exchange program. He has published extensively on media policy, campaign finance and other public policy issues.

Danny Schechter (Common Dreams)

Danny Schechter is a television producer and independent filmmaker who also writes and speaks about media issues. He is the author of *Falun Gong's Challenge to China* (Akashic Press), *The More You Watch, The Less You Know* (Seven Stories Press) and *News Dissector: Passions, Pieces and Polemics* (Electron Press). He is the executive editor of the *MediaChannel.org*, the world's largest on-line media issues network.

Jeff Jarvis (BuzzMachine)

Jeff Jarvis is former TV critic for *TV Guide* and *People*, creator of *Entertainment Weekly*, Sunday editor and associate publisher of the *NY Daily News*, and a columnist on the *San Francisco Examiner*. He was until recently president & creative director of *Advance.net*, the online arm of Advance Publications. Now he is working as editor of a new news startup, still in stealth. He is working with The New York Times Company at *About.com* on content development and strategy and consulting for Advance and Fairchild. He is associate professor and director of the interactive journalism program the City University of New York's new Graduate School of Journalism. He is a columnist for *Media Guardian*. He says he is at work on a book.

Kelly McBride (Poynteronline)

Kelly McBride is an award-winning reporter for *The Spokesman-Review* (Spokane, Wash.), where for 14 years she covered the religion and ethics beat and the police beat. She is currently Poynter Ethics Fellow.

THE INFORMED CITIZEN SERIES

Ever think you may have missed something? *The Informed Citizen Series* aims to collect and present the best of what bloggers have written on U.S. political and social issues. Each book focuses on a specific topic and threads together some of the finest reporting and commentary available on the Internet.

IN THIS SERIES:

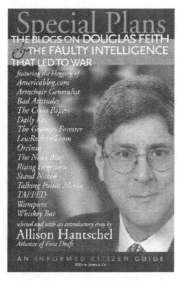

SPECIAL PLANS: the blogs on Douglas Feith and the faulty intelligence that led to war selected and introduced by Allison Hantschel (Athenae of *First Draft*) ISBN: 1-59028-049-9 134 pages, $10.00 U.S.

"Invaluable insight into a key figure behind the propaganda campaign that swayed Americans to support Bush's Iraq War."
—Mark Karlin, Editor and Publisher, *BuzzFlash.com*

ALSO AVAILABLE:

UNTIDY: the blogs on Rumsfeld
Featuring Riverbend (*Baghdad Burning*), Tom Engelhardt (*TomDispatch.com*), Digby (*Hullabaloo*), Jeanne d'Arc (*Body and Soul*), Jeralyn Merritt (*TalkLeft*), Barbara O'Brien (*The Mahablog*), and many more. Selected and introduced by Tom Sumner, series editor.

FREE SHIPPING IN THE CONTINENTAL U.S. ON ORDERS PLACED AT WWW.WMJASCO.COM.